THE
OLD BALL GAME

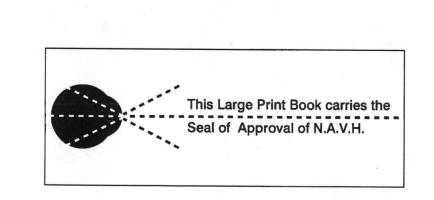

This Large Print Book carries the
Seal of Approval of N.A.V.H.

THE OLD BALL GAME

How John McGraw,
Christy Mathewson,
and the New York Giants
Created Modern Baseball

FRANK DEFORD

Thorndike Press • Waterville, Maine

Published in 2005 by arrangement with Grove Atlantic, Inc.

Thorndike Press® Large Print Nonfiction.

The tree indicium is a trademark of Thorndike Press.

The text of this Large Print edition is unabridged.
Other aspects of the book may vary from the original edition.

Set in 16 pt. Plantin by Liana M. Walker.

Printed in the United States on permanent paper.

Library of Congress Cataloging-in-Publication Data

Deford, Frank.
    The old ball game : how John McGraw, Christy
    Mathewson, and the New York Giants created modern
    baseball / by Frank Deford. — Large print ed.
        p. cm.
    ISBN 0-7862-7660-6 (lg. print : hc : alk. paper)
    1. New York Giants (Baseball team) — History.
    2. McGraw, John Joseph, 1873–1934. 3. Mathewson,
    Christy, 1880–1925. 4. Baseball — United States —
    History.   I. Title.
    GV875.N42D42 2005
    796.357′64′097471—dc22   2005006286

For Sterling Lord

As the Founder/CEO of NAVH, the only national health agency solely devoted to those who, although not totally blind, have an eye disease which could lead to serious visual impairment, I am pleased to recognize Thorndike Press* as one of the leading publishers in the large print field.

Founded in 1954 in San Francisco to prepare large print textbooks for partially seeing children, NAVH became the pioneer and standard setting agency in the preparation of large type.

Today, those publishers who meet our standards carry the prestigious "Seal of Approval" indicating high quality large print. We are delighted that Thorndike Press is one of the publishers whose titles meet these standards. We are also pleased to recognize the significant contribution Thorndike Press is making in this important and growing field.

Lorraine H. Marchi, L.H.D.
Founder/CEO
NAVH

* Thorndike Press encompasses the following imprints: Thorndike, Wheeler, Walker and Large Print Press.

There's only one Christy I know at all,
One Christy I ever saw.
He's the one that discovered
the fadeaway ball
And he pitches for Muggsy McGraw.

— Ring Lardner

ONE

Although neither one of them ever seems to have mentioned it for posterity, John J. McGraw and Christopher Mathewson must surely have first encountered each other on the warm afternoon of Thursday, July 19, in the year 1900, at the Polo Grounds in the upper reaches of Manhattan on an occasion when, as was his wont, McGraw made an ass of himself.

Inasmuch as people at that time were more correct and less impatient than they would be a hundred years later, that summer of 1900 was taken as the last year of an old century rather than the first of a new one. For purposes of symbolism this was good, for it wouldn't be until two years later, in the genuinely new twentieth century, that McGraw and Mathewson would start to work together in New York, there to have such a profound effect upon their sport that they would raise it to a new eminence in the first city of the land, and then beyond, into Americana.

How odd it was, too, how much Mathewson and McGraw achieved together, for never were two men in sport so close to one another and yet so far apart in ilk and personality. Well, maybe that was why they were good for baseball, because they offered us both sides of the coin. Mathewson was golden, tall, and handsome, kind and educated, our beau ideal, the first all-American boy to emerge from the field of play, while McGraw was hardscrabble shanty Irish, a pugnacious little boss who would become the model for the classic American coach — a male version of the whore with a heart of gold — the tough, flinty so-and-so who was field-smart, a man's man his players came to love despite themselves. Every American could want to be Christy Mathewson; every American could admire John J. McGraw.

Nevertheless, that midsummer's day at the Polo Grounds, when the two young men first saw each other, it was not a formal meeting. McGraw might not have even noticed Mathewson, who was what was then called a "debutante" — a raw rookie, just arrived in the National League only a week or so beforehand. Still only nineteen years old, the pitcher had enjoyed an absolutely spectacular tenure at Norfolk in the Virginia League. There, in barely half a season, he had won twenty games while losing only two. The Giants had paid the princely sum of fifteen hundred dollars to purchase young Mathewson, but his initial appearance two days previous, on Tuesday, July 17, had been an abject disaster. At Washington Park in Brooklyn, against the defending champion Superbas, he was sent in to relieve Ed Doheny who, according to one unforgiving newspaper account, "hardly had the strength to get the ball to the plate." Well, to give the devil his due, it was estimated to be 110 degrees down on the diamond. Notwithstanding, the last straw for Doheny was when he allowed a Brooklyn runner to steal third "while he was collecting his thoughts and looking for a breeze."

Out went the call to bring in the "phenom" from the bull pen. Several reporters noted that Mathewson showed some speed, but alas, nothing else. In his first full inning, he gave up five runs. Altogether, in a bit more than three innings pitched, he hit three batters, threw a wild pitch, and allowed four hits while watching his woebegone teammates "go up in the air," butchering various routine chances.

The latter was, however, standard procedure for the Giants. Of special note was the third baseman, "Piano Legs" Charley Hickman, who set a season's record for errors at the hot corner — ninety-one — a mark in ignominy that survives to this day. But then, the New-Yorks were an all-around terrible team, a "baseball menagerie," in last place with a 23–43 record. Newspapers seemed to all but keep in type such headlines as: NEW-YORKS BEATEN AS USUAL and SECOND CLASS BASEBALL IN HARLEM. Indeed, Mathewson had been given a choice by the Norfolk owner — who also had offers from Philadelphia and Cincinnati for his young star — and Matty had chosen New York precisely because the Giants were so weak. Indeed, so dreadful was the team that few observers could bring themselves to call such diamond pygmies Giants. More often they were referred to as the "Harlemites," in recognition of their locale, or the "Tammany Hall team" in honor of their owner, Andrew Freedman, who was an important operative in that corrupt machine. Thus, while Mathewson had correctly concluded that his chances to play would be better in New York, the Harlemites were far worse and more star-crossed than he could possibly have bargained for.

Mathewson joined them in New York after the Giants' return from a particularly disastrous western road trip. In St. Louis, one stalwart, first baseman "Dirty Jack" Doyle, had even been arrested for assaulting the umpire while the "fair-minded spectators yelled 'Shame!' " The Giants were so riven with dissent that as soon as the team staggered back to New York, the manager, Buck Ewing, tendered his resignation. Freedman, the owner, thereupon chose as Ewing's successor George Davis, the very player who led the clique that had refused to give their best for Ewing. Now, as the fresh-faced Mathewson arrived, much of the other half of the team quit on Davis.

Freedman himself was the most hated man in the sport, a distinction he had labored hard to achieve. Bill James, the baseball historian, refers to Freedman as "George Steinbrenner on quaaludes, with a touch of Al Capone." Nobody could work for him. Davis was his fifteenth manager in six years. Hardly any "cranks" (as fans were called till about this time) would travel up to Harlem to see Freedman's team play. Attendance at the Polo Grounds was usually referred to as a "handful." After being on the road for two weeks, only eight hundred showed up to see the team play its first game back, with Mathewson on the roster. The *Tribune* found even those sorts of numbers startling, calling Giant supporters "hoodwinked." So the paper's baseball reporter offered some explanation: "Many strangers find themselves in New-York every day and some of them continue to wander up to this mismanaged institution at the Polo Grounds [where Boss] Croker unearthed 'Andy' Freedman and permitted him to get the fingers of the strangler upon the throat of professional baseball" in New York.

Welcome to the big time, Mr. Mathewson.

On July 16, the day before his debut on the mound (or the "pitcher's box," as it was more commonly referred to), when the Giants played Brooklyn, Mathewson even got to enjoy his first baseball riot. Although the *World* was not impressed by the imbroglio, calling it "a touch of farce-comedy," it had seemed sufficiently threatening for twenty-three of New York's finest to have been called to the ballyard to protect the umpire. After all, "Dirty Jack" Doyle had been released from the St. Louis hoosegow, and you couldn't be too sure. Then, the very next day, Mathewson got shelled in his debut, where upon who should come to town but the St. Louis Cardinals. For reasons lost to antiquity, the New York sports writers enjoyed referring to the Redbird aviary as "the Terrors." Well, perhaps it was all because of their bellicose third baseman, the luminous Mr. McGraw.

Ah, there one can imagine young Christy Mathewson before the game, sneaking a peek at McGraw as he came out onto the field to warm up. He may not have been easy to spot right away. Whereas Mathewson himself was a towering six-feet-two, McGraw was only five-feet, six-and-a-half inches tall; not for nothing would he be known as "The Little Napoleon." He was pasty-faced, too, with light blue eyes — "slitty little cold, gray eyes" someone who disliked him thought — but as a young man he offered up almost a sweet countenance in repose. He wore his coiffure fashionably swirled on the sides in what was known then as the "fishhook effect." Not to put too fine an Irish point on it, but McGraw looked like a leprechaun without a conscience.

Probably, as Matty eyed him, "Muggsy" was horsing around with Wilbert Robinson, "Uncle Robbie," his pal and business partner from their days together in Baltimore. Still, if McGraw was hollering and razzing, as he usually was, Mathewson might not have heard him across the diamond. Muggsy didn't possess a foghorn. Rather, as his wife remembered: "John's voice was light and pitched rather high." But, she added: "It was hairpin sharp."

Mathewson, like so many young baseball players, held McGraw in awe. He had not only been one of the stars of the most glamorous team of the century, the Baltimore Orioles, but McGraw was both the soul and brains of that brazen outfit. A couple years before, as captain of his town team back in Pennsylvania, Mathewson had proudly used a stratagem that he had read that McGraw had dreamed up for the Orioles. "I worshiped him in those days," Mathewson would write years later, "little thinking that I should ever know him; and it was beyond my fondest dreams that I should ever play ball for him."

And here he was — the fabled "Muggsy" McGraw — coming out to take batting practice on the same diamond where Mathewson cowered to the side, eyeing him. McGraw was, by then, probably the most famous athlete in America, his renown the measure of James J. Jeffries, the heavyweight champ. His fame had grown all during the Gay Nineties as he led the Orioles to three championships. He was still only twenty-seven, but had already lived life full. Not only had he spent a decade playing in the majors, he had become a successful manager as well. He was, too, already widowed, and had barely escaped death himself from typhoid fever. He had played ball in Cuba — "El Mono Amarillo," they called him with delight: "the Yellow Monkey" — and had traveled to England and the Continent in style. On the town, where he often sallied forth, McGraw favored shirts and shoes from Cuba to go with one of his blue serge suits that every gentleman then wore all year round. He and his buddy Robinson were prominent Baltimore citizens, owners of the famous Diamond Café, where the sporting gentry of the Monumental City drank, ate, played billiards, and bowled midst handsome oak furnishings. Indeed, so successful was McGraw that when the Orioles franchise had been folded the year before, after the '99 season, he had pretty much called his own tune.

He deigned to go to St. Louis, with the portly Robinson — "his avoirdupois partner" — for only a one-year contract of ten thousand dollars, the highest in the game, and an unprecedented under-the-table arrangement that he and Uncle Robbie would not be bound by the game's reserve clause. That is, once the season was over, the two gentlemen proprietors of the Diamond Café would be free to sign with whomever they pleased. Some McGrawologists figured Muggsy must surely have been angling to take the St. Louis manager's job away from Oliver Wendell "Patsy" Tebeau, but McGraw laughed at that. In his own cockeyed scuffler's style, he explained: "Why, I had more scraps with Patsy than any other man. As a result, we were close friends." No, after the 1900 sojourn in St. Louis, Muggsy wanted to return to some team on the East Coast — ideally to a newly constituted Baltimore nine.

McGraw was still a whale of a player. In '99, even as he had also managed Baltimore, McGraw had hit .391. With St. Louis, although he was just going through the motions, he batted .344 for the 1900 season, leading off and playing third. And so here is young Christy Mathewson, in his first week in the major leagues, eyeballing the famous McGraw's every move, and in the second inning — just the second inning! — Matty watches aghast as Muggsy throws a conniption fit.

Contemporary accounts don't explain what upset McGraw so. We only know that it was a decision at first base. He alone appears to have taken umbrage. Nobody could figure out why. "It was apparent that the decision was imminently correct," the *Times* assured its readers. Umpire Terry finally had enough, though, and ejected McGraw, a dismissal, observed the *Tribune*, "that seemed to dishearten the other members of the St. Louis team." Indeed, with McGraw expelled, the Giants garnered a rare victory, beating the Terrors 8–3. Only then, in defeat, did the losers appear to come to life again "when they applied uncalled for verbal abuse to the umpire."

So did Matty first encounter Muggsy. Probably, as he went back to his room at the Colonial Hotel on 125th Street, he wondered what possibly could have set McGraw off. But then, that's the sort of thing Mathewson might have pondered often for the rest of his baseball life. Sometimes Muggsy just blew his top because that's what Muggsy did. You never could be sure, though. Sometimes he would feign anger and get himself thrown out of a game early on so that he could go to the horse races. That might account for his actions on that particular Thursday, July 19, 1900. St. Louis was out of the pennant race, and the crowd at the Polo Grounds was a handful. The best umpires were on to his scam, though. One time in St. Louis when McGraw pretended to argue a call so vociferously as to get tossed so he could head over to the track, umpire Tim Hurst just smiled at him and said: "There ain't a chance, Mac." No matter how vile and animated Muggsy got with Hurst, the ump just grinned back. McGraw's punishment was that he had to stay and play whether he liked it or not.

Anyway, two weeks after the Polo Grounds ejection, the Giants played in St. Louis. Matty had been rocked again in Pittsburgh the week before, giving up six runs in the first inning he worked in relief. Then, in St. Louis on Saturday, August 4, Mathewson actually pitched to McGraw. Although it's unclear from the box scores exactly when he relieved "Doughnut Bill" Carrick, he came on fairly early, and since McGraw got two hits in the game, at least one and maybe both came off the debutante. St. Louis won 9–8. If Mathewson had any consolation, he did get his first major league hit in this game, a triple. He was always a pretty fair-hitting pitcher.

But unfortunately in 1900 he wasn't much of a pitching pitcher. Manager Davis used him only three more times before the parsimonious Freedman sent Mathewson back to Norfolk so that the owner might get a refund on the deal. On the year with the Giants, Mathewson had no wins but three losses, giving up thirty-four hits, twenty walks, and thirty-two runs in thirty-four innings pitched. He grew terribly homesick living alone at the Colonial Hotel, and on the road nobody in either of the team's two disputatious cliques seemed to have much time for the kid. By the end of the season Mathewson had decided that he was not good enough to make it in baseball. He considered a career in forestry or in the Presbyterian ministry, which is what his mother had in mind for him.

McGraw, too, could hardly wait for the '00 season to end. The Terrors finished tied for fifth, and as soon as the last game was played, McGraw and his avoirdupois partner were on the first train outta town, back to Baltimore, there again to greet their friends at the Diamond Café. As their railroad car crossed over the Mississippi River, Muggsy pulled down the window and he and Uncle Robbie chucked their St. Louis uniforms into the water. Already, McGraw had a pretty good idea of what other fish he would fry. By now he knew that there was going to be a second major league, titled the American, in 1901, and Baltimore was sure to get a franchise.

Meanwhile, Connie Mack, owner and manager of the new Philadelphia team in the upstart league, had heard good things about the debutante Mathewson and offered him a contract of fifteen hundred dollars. Mathewson, growing bold, asked for fifty dollars more, which Mack sent him as a cash advance. For now, forestry and preaching were put on the back burner. However, it would take a year and a half and considerable machinations more before Matty and Muggsy would be back on the field at the Polo Grounds, this time together, there soon to set the world on its ear.

TWO

Looking back from a vantage point of twenty-five years, the historian Mark Sullivan noted "some minor distinctive institutions" that were evident at the turn of the twentieth century in the United States of America. These included: "a national holiday known as Thanksgiving, rocking-chairs, a greater fastidiousness about personal cleanliness as measured by the commonness of bathtubs . . . ice-water, pie, New England boiled dinner, chewing gum." There was a Ping-Pong craze on at that time, and croquet was still all the rage, but Sullivan chose to mention two other games. One was poker, "a diversion . . . indigenous to this nation and containing definite elements of the interplay of psychology not found in ordinary card games." The other was: "baseball, a game calling for unusually quick reactions intellectually, and prompt and easy co-operation muscularly."

In other words, Americans didn't just

play stuff, indoor or out; they were an ingenious folk who naturally favored games that required inordinate intelligence. This seemed to matter. It certainly did to McGraw, who was always going on about how much brainwork baseball needed (which also suggested, by extension, that a manager of such an intellectual enterprise had to be truly bright). Mathewson didn't have to talk about it; he was universally known to be smart as a whip.

Of course, all the cultural analyzing aside, the games that a people favor are those that they find the most fun. But baseball certainly did possess certain ingredients that had made it what *everybody* called it then: the American national sport. First of all, it was a team game, requiring that "prompt and easy co-operation muscularly." As the *Baltimore Morning Herald* rhapsodized: "The *fin de siecle* players must possess a high order of brains, must be of correct habits, have plenty of ambition and be possessed of a certain docility and evenness of temperament such as will insure proper discipline and the frictionless working together of the whole team."

However, peculiar to most team games, baseball features a distinct individual subset, where every batter has a mano a mano confrontation with the pitcher — a *turn* at bat. This neatly satisfied both the unique American organizational talent — it wasn't cowboys that settled the West, it was wagon trains — along with the role for that idealized American individual, the lone wolf.

Moreover, at a time when most Americans labored at long, enervating hours, six days a week of ten-hour workdays, it helped, too, that baseball was not so physically demanding as the back-and-forth team sports. It is certainly no coincidence that at this time, American football, a mean, grueling diversion, was a game played for the most part — and at the highest level of proficiency — by college boys who otherwise were lifting nothing heavier than textbooks. Indeed, the sport was dominated by the wealthiest young gentlemen of all, from the Ivy League. These young gallants not only had the energy to engage in such a demanding activity, but they also could use football to show off, proving that they were every bit as tough as the working classes. Thus, while it is ironic, it is perfectly understandable why baseball, the softer (and, allegedly, more intellectual) game, became a professional entertainment while football, which is so much more gladiatorial, remained essentially an amateur distraction, played primarily by students, for many more years.

Baseball grew up largely in New York and Brooklyn (when it was a city unto itself) strictly as a middle-class amusement — white collar, as we would say today. Its popular increase was viewed as a Good Thing for America. Indeed, in some respects it wasn't so much that Americans played as it was that Americans were *improved* by baseball — perhaps especially the immigrants and other lowlife who had to be educated in this new uplifting way of life on earth. Do-gooders from Jane Addams to the only contemporary American cardinal, James Gibbons of Baltimore, attributed qualities of spirit and cohesion to baseball. Playing it bound us and lifted us alike. Wrote Edwin G. Burrows and Mike Wallace, New York historians: "The spread of baseball, some thought, was a triumph of the civilizing process." Baseball, like Emily Post later on, taught you how to behave middle-class.

Neither was baseball itself modest about its uplifting — and all-American — qualities. Wrote *Spalding's Official Base Ball Guide* in 1888: "It is very questionable

26

whether there is any public sport in the civilized portion of the world so eminently fitted for the people it was made for as the American national game of base ball. In every respect it is an outdoor sport admirably adapted for our mercurial population. It is full of excitement, is quickly played, and it not only requires vigor of constitution and a healthy physique, but manly courage, steady nerve [and] plenty of pluck."

(And where *did* pluck go? It was such a wonderfully American quality of that time.)

Of course, why it was that baseball and football caught on in the Republic instead of cricket and soccer is one of America's more enduring sweet mysteries. Unfortunately, de Tocqueville had passed on by then, so we can't ever be sure. The simplest explanation has to do with proficiency. Baseball and football (and later basketball) require more dexterous skill. There are no 6-4-3 double plays in cricket, and the most adroit soccer player in the World Cup can't do with his feet what a run-of-the-mill junior high football or basketball player can manage with his hands. Proficiency mattered so to a nation on the make.

On the other hand, probably the most intriguing thing about baseball's success is that the sport depends primarily on eyesight. The greatest athletes in the world in terms of speed, strength, and dexterity aren't worth a hill of beans on the diamond if they lack hand-eye coordination. John McGraw signed Jim Thorpe for the Giants, and he was a bust precisely because he couldn't hit a ball that curved — never mind all the other stuff he could do better than anybody else on earth. Although pitchers do not require the same level of ocular acumen as hitters, spotting a pitch — control — is crucial. It's art. Mathewson, who was also a fabulous football player, understood very well. "A pitcher is not a ballplayer," he declared.

But for whatever reasons, baseball caught on in America. Cricket had had its chances, too. The first cricket club in New York was founded in 1839, while the Knickerbocker Base Ball Club didn't begin playing games at Madison and Twenty-seventh Street until three years later. And cricket maintained something of a following even into the twentieth century. Perhaps it tells us more about how little the first World Series mattered, when Boston played Pittsburgh in 1903, but notwithstanding, in the *New York Times*, the newspaper of record, the first game of the first Series was simply listed under a roundup headline that read: YESTERDAY'S BASEBALL GAMES, while the larger headline on that same sports page concerned a match on Staten Island, which was: ENGLISH CRICKETERS WIN.

Surely, too, something of the popularity of baseball (and football) had to do with the fact that, whatever their English antecedents, they were indigenous American games. Curiously, the favored *individual* spectator sports that caught on in the latter part of the nineteenth century — horse racing, boxing, tennis, golf, and track — had all more or less been transported from the British Isles and were quickly accepted here. But, by golly, we needed our own team games. Soccer aficionados in particular, of course, have never gotten over the fact that their sport is number one virtually everywhere in the world except in the U.S., but the fact is that it just never caught the fancy of Americans. Of course, it is an article of faith every year that *next year* America will redeem itself and catch up with the universal taste and embrace soccer as a spectator worship. 'SOCKER' FOOTBALL GROWS IN FAVOR headlined a story in the *New York Herald* during the 1905 World Series. Such a story might have been run, wistfully, every October since then.

But baseball was the team game that began to rule. Early on, Union troops spread the sport during the Civil War, and afterward, whether in the farmlands or in the great cities that began to explode with the industrial revolution, baseball became the American game of the American dream. Especially for any minority boy seeking inclusion, baseball was the key to membership. As late as 1923, in one of the dandiest paeans to fellowship extant, the *Sporting News* (which was always called "the Bible of baseball") warmly boasted this scripture: "The Mick, the Sheeny, the Wop, the Dutch and the Chink, the Indian, the Jap or the so-called Anglo-Saxon — his nationality is never a matter of moment if he can pitch, hit or field."

(Of course, notably lacking from that friendly roster is the African-American, who had been excluded from "organized" baseball by 1880. As vulgar and common as the *Sporting News*' ethnic references might be, it is worth noting that even two years later, in 1925, the *New Yorker*, that bible of sophistication, wrote that when

McGraw got rid of a popular player, he had "sold [him] down the river like any common field nigger.")

So baseball embraced and even elevated its participants, and it provided common amusement for the citizenry. In 1869 the Cincinnati Red Stockings became the first professional team (although staffed with many New Yorkers), and soon thereafter, in the 1870s, leagues began to bloom. So much of baseball's unique heritage developed so quickly: trades of players, the reserve clause, player unions and strikes, major leagues and minor leagues, large markets and small markets. Beer made an early alliance with baseball, especially in cities with considerable German populations, where the brewery barons caught on quickly that games played in the sunshine made the ideal place to sell their suds to the cranks sitting in the hot bleachers (so named, of course, because the hot sun bleached the wood).

Baltimore, Cincinnati, Louisville, Philadelphia, and Pittsburgh all had franchises backed by beer money, and Christian Frederick Wilhelm Von der Ahe, known as "Der Boss President," owner of the St. Louis Brown Stockings, was so far ahead of his time that he had largely been for-

31

gotten when Bill Veeck came along many decades later to put a new shine on Von der Ahe's ideas. In order to increase crowds and sell beer, Der Boss President offered fireworks, oompah bands, merry-go-rounds, water slides, horse races, Wild West shows, special trolley cars, a stadium club, ladies' sections, and, of course, a *biergarten.* Only bobblehead dolls avoided Der Boss President's prescience.

But baseball, then as now, was always struggling not to screw up a good thing. It seems amazing now, at a time when all leagues the world over feature a *postseason* that almost seems as inclusive and enduring as the *regular* season itself, but the idea of playoffs and divisions pretty much eluded the owners. Not only that, but as late as 1899, the National League — then the only major league — had twelve teams. As a consequence, there was one winner and eleven losers, many of whom were eliminated from serious consideration by the holiday at the end of May, then called Decoration Day.

The Cleveland Spiders of 1899 are often cited for their spectacular ineptitude, finishing eighty-four games behind the Brooklyn Superbas, with a 20–134 record, but inglorious losers were the order of the decade. Moreover, some teams had no long-term hope whatsoever because of what was called "syndicate baseball," wherein one owner owned two teams. He would stock one of his two teams with most of the best players, so essentially what developed was a situation where some of the so-called major league teams were really minor league farm clubs. Even for the better teams that had nothing to point to at the end of the season, it's rather amazing that interest and attendance held up as well as it did.

Baseball also suffered two blows it had no control over in the 1890s. The financial panic of '93 and the Spanish-American War of '98 both kept down the crowds and threatened the lives of whole franchises. On a sustaining basis, though, the decline of Andrew Freedman's Giants from mediocrity to embarrassment hurt all of professional baseball, because with a laughingstock of a team in the nation's biggest city, the sport lacked the national spotlight that only McGraw and Mathewson would finally bring to it at the dawn of the new century.

Freedman had purchased the Giants for forty-eight thousand dollars in 1895, right after the club finished second, trailing only

McGraw and the Orioles. An Indianapolis department store magnate, John Brush — "the Hoosier Wanamaker" he was called — had also sought to purchase the Giants. Freedman attacked Brush in the bar of the Fifth Avenue Hotel before a friend of Brush stepped in and walloped Freedman. Nonetheless, he got the team and soon alienated everybody. He did not help his press relations by punching out a *Times* reporter and regularly barring his many and sundry newspaper critics from the ballpark. Freedman was good-looking. Also: cheap, impulsive, and disagreeable — "utterly lacking in tact" — but he was prominent in Tammany and quick to blame his friendlessness on anti-Semitism.

One time in 1898 at the Polo Grounds, a former Giant named Ducky Holmes, then playing for the Orioles, got into some dispute with a member of the home team and, as a final fillip, screamed: "At least I'm not working for a sheeny anymore." Freedman heard the slur and went berserk, and when the umpire wouldn't punish Holmes for his outburst, the Giant owner ordered his team off the field, forfeiting. The truth of the matter, though, was that when it came to Andrew Freedman, the animating emotion was not anti-Semitism but anti-

Freedmanism. Jews didn't like him any better than anybody else, and he was so generally despised that that antipathy was transposed upon the whole Giant franchise.

The fact is, what prejudice there was in baseball as the nineteenth century wound down was generally directed against the Irish. They predominated on the diamond and, in fact, had been prominently involved in the sport since its earliest years. In 1858 the Waspy Knickerbockers had consented to play a series against an Irish team from Brooklyn called Po Reilly's, and crowds of thousands had showed up despite a fifty-cent admission fee. Over time, "The Sons of Erin," as the *Sporting News* invariably called them, had come to play so large a role in professional baseball that there developed the same sort of backlash against the Irish in baseball as, say, was directed at blacks in the 1970s when they began to dominate the National Basketball Association. Well into the 1890s, probably up to 40 percent of major league players were of Irish descent.

The Irish themselves were, naturally, not only proud of their preeminence, but convinced that they did indeed have a special aptitude for the game. In 1896, Bill Joyce, one of Andrew Freedman's revolving-door Giant managers, offered this assessment (which pretty much was the consensus wisdom of that time): "Give me a good Irish infield, and I will show you a good team. . . . You want two or three quick-thinking sons of Celt to keep the Germans and the others moving. . . . Get an Irishman to do the scheming. Let him tell the Germans what to do, and then you will have a great combination." (Good Lord, but the Germans must have been slowpokes; most every contemporary reference cackles at their lack of foot speed.)

The Sons of Erin included some dandy ballplayers. The first major baseball celebrity was an Irish-American named Mike Kelly. He was, however, always called "King." He was also christened "the $10,000 Beauty" because the Boston team, known as the Beaneaters (still, surely, the worst nickname in the annals of sport), paid that vast amount to the Chicago White Stockings in 1887 to purchase Kelly. He was thus in Boston at about the time John L. Sullivan became another Irish hero, as heavyweight champion. Sullivan, the Boston Strongboy, was something of a lout. Champion he might be but, for lack of a better word, he was fat. He wolfed down bourbon from beer steins, bellowing "I can lick any sonuvabitch in the house" in whatever saloon he stomped into.

King Kelly was no less a stranger to John Barleycorn, but he was a stylish dude, favoring London-tailored suits, a tall silk hat, jeweled ascot, and patent leather shoes "as sharply pointed as Italian dirks." His Hub fans gave him a carriage drawn by two white horses so that he might ride to the park in proper style, and there they would cry out in unison:

Slide, Kelly, slide.
Slide, Kelly, slide.
Slide, Kelly, on your belly —
Slide, Kelly, slide.

The King did slide. He invented the hook slide. He could hit, too — .308 lifetime. He also was famous for ducking across the infield when the sole umpire's attention was diverted, going from first to third diagonally. Once, when he was sitting out a game with a hangover, a pop foul headed near the Beaneater bench. Seeing that the catcher could not reach the ball, Kelly stood up, screamed "Kelly now catching for Boston," and caught the ball. The startled umpire had to allow the ploy, for there had been nothing in the rule book to anticipate such an instant substitution (although a new rule was quickly inserted to close the King's loophole).

Kelly was so popular that other teams were afraid he was going to drag salaries up to insupportable levels, and so the league instituted a $2,000 salary cap. The King threatened to quit and become a music hall performer full-time, so the Beaneaters circumvented the new league rule by paying him the $2,000 maximum legal salary, but giving him an additional $3,000 for the use of his photograph in advertising. Alas, Kelly never could outrun liquor. He was ordered to take Turkish baths before every game to get the booze out of his system, but the fine, hard living caught up with him. King Kelly died in 1894, before his thirty-seventh birthday.

If Kelly was the image of the carousing Irish ballplayer, that model was, of course, hardly universal. The spare, ascetic Cornelius McGillicuddy, who as Connie Mack would become McGraw's greatest managerial rival, stood in stark contrast. "Voiceless Jim" O'Rourke was also every Irishman's hero. When it was proposed that he drop the "O" from his name so that he might better fit with a predominantly

Protestant team, O'Rourke refused, declaiming: "I would rather die than give up my father's name. A million dollars would not tempt me." And on he went to Yale Law School, to learn to bloviate full-time for a living.

But it was the Baltimore Orioles who were to make the most pronounced mark upon the game in the nineteenth century. They were Irish and played a roughhouse brand of baseball that split the game. As the young and innocent Christy Mathewson grew up in bucolic Factoryville, Pennsylvania, and then moved on to study nearby at Bucknell College, the fabulous tales of the Orioles, of Joe Kelley and Hughie Jennings and Wee Willie and Uncle Robbie and Muggsy McGraw, reached him and brought him great wonder.

THREE

John McGraw arrived in Baltimore on August 24, 1891. "Just get me out there and watch my smoke," he advised the startled manager, who was expecting a somewhat more impressive package. McGraw was eighteen years old, and not only was he short, he weighed only 121 pounds. He had such short arms that when he came into some money, he began to have his suits tailored so that the sleeves would not hang down, foolishly, to his palms. The Orioles, who seemed "to have had more trouble with its players getting drunk than any other club," were amused by the little busher just in from Iowa and, as he sat on the bench during his first game, they pushed him off. He came up off the ground windmilling, ready to take on the whole kit and caboodle.

So began McGraw's big league career. It would last, uninterrupted, for more than forty years. However, he began only somewhat more auspiciously on the field as on the bench, batting .270 for the season and making twenty-one errors in only ninety-eight chances. The next year offered little improvement, but the Orioles paid him only twelve hundred dollars and sometimes pressed him into service as a ticket-taker, so he escaped, with pleadings, from being farmed out to Mobile. He was desperate to stay in Baltimore once he got there.

It wasn't just the baseball. For a small-town kid from upstate New York, Baltimore absolutely dazzled him. H. L. Mencken, the sage of Baltimore, was eleven years old when McGraw came to town, but later he had decided: "Baltimore, by 1890, was fast disintegrating, and so was civilization." Mencken held no more regard for McGraw's occupation. "I hate all sports," he once wrote, "as rabidly as a person who likes sports hates common sense."

But to the youthful McGraw, Baltimore and the Orioles were rapture. The city itself, sixth largest in the nation, approaching half a million souls, was a lively amalgamation, the border entrepôt between North and South. It was still a lot of Dixie. In 1894 a dark-complected outfielder named George Treadway was traded from the Orioles to Brooklyn because he was razzed so often from the stands, with mean shouts that he was a black man. Baltimore was at least somewhat cosmopolitan, though, and earthy, a sailor's town, offering the naughty delights of any port. It was also big on horse racing; here McGraw found the ponies he would bet the rest of his life. One-fourth of the population was German — naturally, the Orioles were owned by a German brewer, Harry von der Horst — but there was a substantial number of blacks and hillbillies, and, continuing Maryland's original designation as a Roman Catholic preserve, Baltimore was a most comfortable place for an Irish boy to find himself.

More important, perhaps, the Orioles' new manager, "Silent Ned" Hanlon, was cleaning house of the drunken old scruff-buckets, cleverly replacing them with young Irish players of the McGravian stripe. They were all a bit older than Muggsy, and although Hanlon was a superb manager, "foxy," whom McGraw admired, and although his pal Uncle Robbie was a popular captain, the kid McGraw became the engine of the team. "Woe betide he who fails us!" Muggsy cried.

The three newcomers whom Hanlon

cadged from other teams would all (like Hanlon and McGraw and Robinson) make the Hall of Fame. They were Hughie Jennings, Joe Kelley, and "Wee Willie" Keeler, and they all lived together at a boardinghouse to the north of town, on York Road. There, it seems, McGraw always appropriated the hammock. The residence was conveniently located about ten minutes from Union Park, where they worked together, and perhaps a similar distance to St. Ann's Church, where they prayed together — often with Silent Ned Hanlon himself leading them to the pews. Later, when McGraw married, he and Uncle Robbie bought adjoining row houses downtown.

McGraw adored his closest teammates. When he wrote his memoirs after more than twenty years in New York with the Giants, it was still the Old Orioles whom he remembered most affectionately. "It is the only [ball club] that remains in spirit a team to this day," he wrote. Well into the twentieth century, the Orioles would hold reunions, like high school and college classes do. For all that New York meant to McGraw, for all the years he lived there, it was Baltimore where he had come of age with his buddies, Baltimore where he would choose to be buried.

The closest of these pals was Hughie Jennings, a freckle-faced Pennsylvania coal miner who had suffered from malaria and was hitting .136, when Hanlon boosted him from Louisville in 1893. McGraw took it upon himself that off-season to correct Jennings's tendency to fall away from inside pitches in fear, "stepping in the bucket." He achieved this by placing Jennings at bat indoors, his back up against a wall, so he simply couldn't bail out when McGraw pitched inside to him. It was, in a way, Muggsy's first managerial triumph. Jennings batted .335 the next season, went as high as .401 in '96, and retired .311 lifetime.

Joe Kelley, a left fielder, was one of Hanlon's earliest acquisitions, coming over from Pittsburgh in 1892. From Cambridge, Massachusetts, he was originally Joe *Kelly*, but added the "e" to foster the impression that he was lace-curtain. At five-feet-eleven, 190 pounds, Kelley was a big man for that era, but what most distinguished him was his looks — a sweet, almost cherubic handsome that left hearts aflutter wherever he played. He was not unaware of his beauty and often carried a small hand mirror into the outfield to check upon his appearance during lulls in the action.

Wee Willie Keeler came to the Orioles in 1894 from Brooklyn, his hometown. He was as sweet as he was tiny. When he died in 1921, the first of the Old Orioles to pass on, age fifty, McGraw was so overcome, looking at his little friend lying there in the casket, that he started bawling so loud that Joe Kelley was obliged to come into the room and roughly pull him away. Keeler claimed to be five-feet, four-and-one-half inches tall, but he did pack 140 pounds. In context, Wee Willie wasn't as wee as he sounds, though, inasmuch as the average ballplayer of this era wasn't much more than five-nine. In the event, Wee Willie made the most of his size, choking up his teeny thirty-inch wand, and then, in his own memorable description: "Keep your eye clear and hit 'em where they ain't." In 1897, when he batted .424, he made hits in his first forty-four games, a record that stood till Joe DiMaggio memorably topped it in 1941.

But it wasn't just that all the Birds could hit. What distinguished the Old Orioles was their camaraderie and clever hijinks. They didn't revolutionize the game, but they surely renovated it. They were tricksters. In fact, their most important partner in crime wasn't the manager, Hanlon, or another player, but the groundskeeper, one Tom Murphy. Working with McGraw and the others, out in front of the plate he mixed dirt with a clay burnt hard. The Orioles would then swing down on the pitch so that the batted ball would hit the concrete-like ground and carom high into the air. By the time the ball came down, the batter would be on first. To this day, that is called the "Baltimore chop."

Murphy also doctored the foul lines between home plate and first or third, slanting them, so that bunts would stay fair. To help the speedy young Birds, the path to first base was canted slightly downhill. Since it was common for pitchers then to reach down off the mound for some dirt to soil their sweaty hands, Murphy larded the dirt in that area with soap chips. Opposing pitchers would suddenly find the spheroid mysteriously slipping from their grasp.

Keeler's right-field bailiwick was the wild kingdom. The field out there sloped down to the fence, so that Wee Willie, playing deep, could sometimes barely be seen from home plate. He negotiated the territory in damp, ankle-deep weeds and grass, where it was possible for him to hide extra balls that could be retrieved and tossed in should the legitimate ball in play get beyond his grasp.

It was, apparently, these Orioles who first designed the strategy of having the pitcher cover first when a ground ball took the first baseman wide of the bag. No one is quite sure who dreamed up the hit-and-run, whereby the runner on first would break for second as if to attempt a steal, drawing the second baseman to the bag, thus leaving a large hole for the batter to slap a pitch through to right field. Some claim that the ploy originated with the Beaneaters in the '80s — very possibly dreamed up by King Kelly himself.

If they did not invent the hit-and-run, though, the Orioles are fairly credited with establishing it as a regular stratagem. McGraw, never afraid to heap credit upon himself, put it this way years later: "If I may be permitted to say so, Keeler and I practically revolutionized the style of hitting to advance the runner, a form of attack that had never been given much attention up to 1894." In particular, the opening series of that season against the Giants not only established the hit-and-run, but was the inspiration that lifted the

Orioles toward glory. This was the moment they found themselves, when they understood all that they were. Starting at this point, Baltimore would win three straight pennants (and then twice finish a close second).

The Giants were then, in the pre-Freedman days, a respectable franchise, favored to win the National League that year of '94 under their manager, John Montgomery Ward. For all the scoundrels and ignoramuses populating baseball then, it also included many characters more fascinating than the incurious plastic figurines who inhabit professional sport today. Ward had been a terrific pitcher, and then, when his arm went bad, he became a shortstop while picking up a law degree at Columbia. He led a players' revolt, was elected president of the new union, the "Brotherhood," and actually started a new league that was a socialist cooperative. But as bright as John Montgomery Ward was, he didn't know what hit him and his Giants when they came to Baltimore to start the '94 season.

After a grand Opening Day parade up stately Charles Street, more than fifteen thousand packed into Union Park. It was the largest crowd ever in Baltimore, and with McGraw leading off and Keeler behind him, the Orioles ran the Giants silly that day and on the two that followed. "Just a lot of horseshoe luck," Ward snorted. Other critics called it "sissy ball." But McGraw and the Baltimoreans sensed the new dawn. "That one series made the Orioles," McGraw would reminisce. Even the mayor was estatic. "We have always had the most beautiful women and the finest oysters in the world," he exclaimed, "and now we have the best baseball club." The grandest of babes, mollusks, and baseball — how much brighter could the sun shine on any one place in God's acreage?

McGraw was in his glory. "Little Mac at third was a whole team and a dog under the wagon," the *Morning Herald* crowed. He was full of tricks and full of himself. "We were a cocky, swashbuckling crew, and we wanted everyone to know it," he recalled. At that time, fouls did not count as strikes, and McGraw had the ability to foul almost any pitch off. Once, he wasted some poor pitcher's best stuff, binging twenty-four straight fouls. In 1930, when he was a fat old man of fifty-six, he picked up a bat in spring training one day and fouled off twenty-six straight pitches. Indeed, it was more because of McGraw than anyone else that the rule would eventually be changed and fouls would start being counted as strikes.

Since only one umpire worked a game, it was possible, simply, to get away with more shenanigans. McGraw's favorite trick, when he was playing third and a runner tagged up there, was to gently hook a finger into the runner's belt. When the fly was caught and the runner started to light out for home, McGraw would be literally holding him on the bag — but in such a fashion that the umpire couldn't see. (One runner, wise to the con, finally outwitted McGraw by quietly unbuckling his belt. McGraw slipped his finger into the belt, the runner took off, the belt unspooled, and there was McGraw standing on third with the opponent's belt in his hand.)

But so much of the Old Oriole spirit wasn't cute. McGraw and a lot of his teammates would put a beefsteak into their shoes to serve as softer innersoles, but it's also true that long before Ty Cobb became famous for it, McGraw would sharpen his spikes with, in his own bloodthirsty boast, "murderous intent." He was loud and abusive, and although he looked back on it all as boys-will-be-boys — "we had more fun with the umpires than we do now," he remembered sweetly — the feeling was not at all mutual.

Umpires were at once fearful of him and out to get him. Never mind players, McGraw would spike umpires. The *Sporting News* wailed: "To be aggressive does not mean to make the life of the umpire miserable and to disgust spectators." After the ump kicked Muggsy out of a game in New York in '95, he grew even more obstreperous, so that the arbiter was obliged to call out the local constabulary to escort McGraw from the premises. The amazing thing is, too, that Muggsy was weak at the time, recovering from malaria. He was unrelenting. Trying to explain him, one umpire allowed that McGraw "eats gunpowder every morning and washes it down with warm blood." In spring training one year, a Macon, Georgia, reporter, encountering McGraw for the first time, was absolutely stunned by what he witnessed: "A rough, unruly man, who is constantly playing dirty ball. He has the vilest tongue of any ball-player. . . . He adopts every low and contemptible method that his erratic brain can conceive to win a play by a dirty trick." Baltimore, which was not known as "Mob Town" for nothing, fed off Muggsy and his cronies. Young Hugh Fullerton, who would become perhaps the most distinguished sportswriter in the land, reported that the Baltimore park "reeked with obscenity and profanity."

So, as glamorous as the Orioles were in their manly way, they soon felt a backlash. Old-time promoters like Chris Von der Ahe in St. Louis, who was known as "half-genius, half-buffoon," thought that baseball had to be rowdy to succeed, but generally the mood was shifting. John Brush, who had unsuccessfully sought to buy the Giants but who now owned the Cincinnati Reds, actually proposed what was called a "purification plan" to try and make baseball more respectable. McGraw was so astounded by that heresy that, disconsolately, he groaned that if such genteel rules were instituted he might have to "abandon my profession entirely."

But any cagey businessman could see that the world was tilting, that respectable women were starting to come out of their houses, and that the future of entertainment lay not with blood and sex but with a more broad-based family appeal. Why, even boxing had given up bare-knuckle fights and put gloves on the likes of John L. Sullivan, and when Teddy Roosevelt got into the White House and finished busting trusts and settling hostilities in the Far East, he called together representatives of Harvard, Yale, and Princeton and all but ordered them to create new football rules that would prohibit the flower of the Ivy League from maiming one another for the amusement of carriage-trade crowds.

Then, too, once the cocky Orioles had been knocked off their perch, it became more difficult for the National League to excuse their roughhouse brand. Baltimore's reign essentially ended late in September of '97, when the Beaneaters came to town and took two out of three games. The series drew 57,000 cranks, with the final game packing in 25,375 — what was surely the largest baseball crowd in history. Boston won 19–10, as the *Baltimore Sun* lamented in language even more florid than was customary in such an embroidered age: "Let us drop a tear and go on, and let it be a hot and scalding tear, for verily Boston is hot stuff, and her beans are smoking. Let her light her bonfires and regild her State House dome and send forth some modern Paul Revere to ride and spread the news."

So the Old Orioles had lost their control of the game. At the same time, popular entertainment was changing. A singer named

Tony Pastor, famous for his renditions of such street hits as "The Strawberry Blonde" and "Lulu, The Beautiful Hebrew Girl," had opened a theater uptown on Union Square in New York in 1885 that promised no blue material. A devout Catholic who dressed in an opera hat, with the kind of handlebar mustache that John McGraw so envied but could never grow, Pastor had created something that would be called vaudeville. It was an immediate hit. Soon, men named Albee and Keith took Pastor's idea onto the road — circuits — seeding family fare throughout America, in all the same places where Muggsy McGraw and his disciples had played baseball with meanness and crudity before crowds of coarse inebriates.

Keith's wife, Mary Catherine, posted rules backstage that left no room for misinterpretation: "You are hereby warned that your act must be free from all vulgarity and suggestiveness in words, action and costume. . . . Such words as Liar, Slob, Son-of-a-Gun, Devil, Sucker, Damn and all other words unfit for the ears of ladies and children . . . are prohibited under fine of instant discharge." And it worked. Vaudeville took off like a rocket while baseball plateaued, as players proudly held on to their old image of hard-drinking, women-chasing rogues.

Eddie Cantor, the vaudeville star, recalled that when he was a boy and he did something mischievous, his grandmother would label him with the worst profession she could think of: "Why, you, you ballplayer you." And it wasn't as if baseball itself wasn't aware of its dubious reputation. The *Spalding Guide* of 1889 bemoaned: "Saloon and brothel . . . are the two greatest obstacles in the way of success of the majority of professional players."

Certainly, as Christy Mathewson finished up his studies at the local academy in Factoryville and began to prepare to matriculate at Bucknell, no one who knew the fine lad from that upstanding family of worthy American stock could expect that he would ever join the debased ranks of baseballists. Why, an infielder named Fred Tenney, who had graduated from Brown and come to the majors in 1894, was, for this, known as "the Soiled Collegian." Walter Camp of Yale, who was sort of the godfather of football, had written thusly on the subject: "You don't need your boy 'hired' by anyone. If he plays, he plays as a gentleman, and not as a professional; he plays for victory, not for money; and whatever bruises he may have in the flesh, his heart is right, and he can look you in the eye, as a gentleman should."

But luckily for young Matty — and, although he would never admit it, luckily for the unregenerate Muggsy, too — a baseball writer from Cincinnati named Byron Bancroft Johnson, who was fat, hard-drinking, and loosely principled — exactly the sort of fellow you would never expect to champion gentility — decided to depart journalism in order to take over the operation of a minor circuit, the Western League. One day, spending time at the Ten-Minute Club on Vine Street in Cincinnati, Johnson had an idea.

It was called the Ten-Minute Club because if you didn't order a new drink every ten minutes, you had to leave. So here it was, at the Ten-Minute Club, that Ban Johnson ordered another whiskey and began to think seriously about decency.

FOUR

While McGraw was playing his last years at Baltimore — split by the season's sojourn in St. Louis — Mathewson was going to college. This was a time when only about 6 percent of the 76 million Americans had graduated from high school. Indeed, in New York, children as young as twelve were allowed to work if they attended merely eighty days of school a year. Many boys didn't bother with even that tacit minimum. They were everywhere — guttersnipes, the proper folk called them — trying to subsist as newsboys and street arabs. In such a society, a college man was someone invariably privileged and always special.

Mathewson's college tenure, however, was simply brilliant. We can understand better why he got so down on himself when he didn't immediately prosper with the Giants in '00, because he had enjoyed nothing but easy success in college. Indeed, from the minute Matty showed up at

Bucknell in Lewisburg, Pennsylvania, and put on his blue freshman beanie in the fall of '98, he did everything, it seems, and all of it well. It was not just sports and his studies, where he earned such marks as 96 in analytic chemistry and German, 94 in Tacitus, and 93 in Horace. He played in the band, sang in the glee club, acted in the dramatic society, participated in the Latin Philosophical, wrote poetry, served on the Junior Ball Committee, was chosen as class historian, and (naturally) made the Leadership Society and was elected class president.

Of course, he starred on the baseball team, but he also jumped center for the basketball varsity and was best known for his football exploits. In fact, Matty professed to enjoy football more than baseball. He was called "the infant phenomenon," or "Rubber Leg," playing fullback and kicking field goals — at a time when a field goal counted five points, almost as much as a touchdown. Apparently he had the same pinpoint control with his right leg on the gridiron as he did with his right arm on the diamond. After he kicked a forty-eight yarder from an acute angle against Army, Walter Camp himself gave Mathewson his benediction, declaring that he was "the greatest drop-kicker in intercollegiate competition."

Thus was Christy Mathewson already the beau ideal in the making, the first all-American boy — or, perhaps more accurately, he was the first flesh-and-blood all-American boy. The honor realistically belonged to a slightly older contemporary, Frank Merriwell of Fardale Academy and then Yale, who was the fictional creation of a hack writer named Gilbert Patten.

For a sixty-dollar payday, Patten conjured up Merriwell in 1896 for the *Tip Top Weekly* — what was called a dime novel. Patten dreamed of being a serious author but was never able to pull that off, at least in some part because he could not manage to write sex with any facility. But Frank was chaste, so that was no problem. So, writing as Burt L. Standish (other Patten noms de plume included Stanton L. Burt, Harry Dangrefield, Julian St. Dare, and Wyoming Will), Patten created young Frank, putting him on the playing fields of Fardale. The author chose the name thusly: Frank, for earnestness and candor; Merry, for disposition; Well, for health and vitality. He envisioned his character as "a new style . . . more in touch with the times." Specifically, Frank Merriwell would be the country's first sports idol. "I saw the opportunity to feature all kinds of athletic sports, with baseball predominating," he would write.

Unfortunately for Patten, Merriwell was more of a success than he ever could have imagined. Like Sherlock Holmes or Tarzan were to become for their authors, Merriwell became an albatross to Patten. He moved him up from the fictional Fardale to the real Yale; he dreamed up an ambidextrous younger brother; he put Frank in this sport and that one, brought in new villains and cliffs to hang from. But on and on went cheerful Frank, from one improbable success to another. Patten would churn out his stories for twenty years until 1916, when the nickelodeon finally put the dime novel out of business and poor Patten out of his misery. For most weeks, all that time, he would spend four days of every week creating a new Merriwell story. Then, relieved, he would spend two days unsuccessfully struggling with sexless adult fiction, finally resting from his labors on the seventh, only to start the process all over again the next week. Frank Merriwell sold 500 million copies before his demise (although he would be resurrected in comic strips, movies, and, as late as 1946–49, as an NBC radio hero).

Specifically, Frank Merriwell became famous for two things. First was his ability to bring home the bacon, to snatch victory from the jaws of defeat, to pull the fat from the fire at the eleventh hour. Fictional he may have been, but he was a living proverb. Indeed, even for much of the first half of the twentieth century, to "pull a Merriwell" became an expression applied to any unlikely last-minute success. But just as important to Frank's image was his good sportsmanship. Victory was never achieved at the expense of honor. His good deeds were manifold, and those many athletic villains who practiced "muckerism," which is what gamesmanship was called then, were sure to get bested by Frank in the last chapter. "He's a regular Frank Merriwell" was the highest accolade a young man could be handed.

Christy Mathewson was a regular Frank Merriwell. Or, almost: Frank Merriwell was a regular Christy Mathewson. Anyway, both were decent, clean-cut, handsome college men, the ideals of what was known as "muscular Christianity." (Teddy Roosevelt might have been lumped with Matty and Frank as the third member of this muscular Christian trinity.) The point was that young Christian men didn't have to be wimps. They won games, but they won them only in Jesus' image, playing by the rules. They were the original WWJD, Sports Division: What Would Jesus Do on the field of play?

At a time when muckerism, as particularly expounded by McGraw himself, was the baseball model, Mathewson was the antidote. American boys and their parents had read how Frank Merriwell could win fair and square in fiction. Now Matty would display those same qualities in real life. It was almost too much a coincidence, but the one failing Patten gave Merriwell to make him marginally human was, in fact, the one discernible weakness that Mathewson fell prey to: he loved to gamble. As one of Mathewson's teammates, Rube Marquard, said: "If you had a dollar in your pocket, Matty would never be satisfied until he got that dollar from you."

Whereas that harsh bit of truth was generally unknown to the legion of Mathewson's worshipers, it's quite possible that many Merriwell anecdotes came, over time, to be attributed to Mathewson. There are tales that umpires would surreptitiously look to Matty on a close play, to get his opinion — a shake or nod of the head — knowing that he would never call it dishonestly, even to benefit his own team. For example, it has been told in diamond scripture that one time when he slid home, he kicked up so much dust the umpire was blinded, so the trusting arbiter simply turned to Mathewson and asked him for the call. "He got me," Mathewson replied straightaway, and only then did the relieved umpire cry, "Out!"

"Why would you admit that?" asked the bewildered catcher.

"Because I am a church elder."

Indeed, there were so many he's-a-regular-Merriwell tales that grew up about Mathewson that, in exasperation, his wife would regularly try to modify the record, Saint Division, saying such things as, "Christy's no goody-goody" and "You really don't think I'd marry such a prude, do you?"

On the other hand, as we shall see, it seems as if Mathewson's word of honor really was, all by itself, what cost his Giants the pennant in 1908.

But if Frank Merriwell and Christy Mathewson diverged in one place, it was that only Christy took filthy lucre to exploit his talent. Most upstanding citizens agreed with Walter Camp and were leery of professional athletes. Jim Thorpe would have to give up his 1912 Olympic gold medals because he had played summer baseball for a few dollars. When Matty was still in college, though, President Roosevelt had not yet forced the National Collegiate Athletic Association into existence, and so Mathewson did nothing illegal when he pitched professionally summers while still playing on the Bucknell teams.

Indeed, in the autumn of '99, a baseball scout named "Phenomenal John" Smith came to Philadelphia, where Mathewson was playing a football game against Penn, intent on offering the sophomore eighty dollars a month to pitch for Norfolk in the Virginia League the next summer. He met with Mathewson before the game, and Matty was set to accept what he considered to be a most opulent offer. In the football game, however, he kicked two field goals, so impressing Phenomenal John that, for no rational reason, the scout upped the *baseball* bid to ninety dollars.

Already, the summer before, after his freshman year, Mathewson had plied his trade for a while in the New England

League, with the team for Taunton, Massachusetts. This was a rather unremarkable interlude, except apparently it was here that Mathewson picked up his famous pitch, the fadeaway, while watching an old-timer mess around with it.

At first Mathewson just called it his "freak pitch." It was thrown with the same grip as his regular curve — which Mathewson himself thought was "my very best [pitch], and a surprise for all the batters." But what distinguished the fadeaway was that it broke in the opposite direction from a curve — in on right-handed batters, away from left-handers. It also seems to have dropped rather dramatically.

Mathewson threw it sort of inside out, so that his palm ended face-up after the ball was released, "twisting off [my] thumb with a peculiar snap of the wrist." Mathewson realized early on that contorting his arm that way had the potential for great injury, so even after he mastered his freak pitch, he limited himself to spotting it only a few times a game. Sure enough, incredibly, despite all that McGraw used him, he virtually never came down with a sore arm.

When Mathewson first came up to the Giants that July of '00, he didn't really consider his freak pitch to be part of his repertoire. But when he was showing his stuff to George Davis, the player-manager, and Davis walloped a couple of Mathewson's regular curves, Matty trotted out the freak pitch. Twice Davis bit, swinging and missing. "That's a good one," he hollered to the debutante. "It's a slow in-curve to a right-handed batter. A regular fallaway, or a fadeaway." Davis encouraged the kid to work on the pitch, which Mathewson did, and once he learned to control it, which was so difficult because of "that peculiar snap of the wrist," the fadeaway became his signature. (Curiously, since most batters are right-handed, the pitch absolutely did *not* fade away from them. On the contrary, it ran in. But Davis was a switch-hitter, and he was obviously taking his cuts that day as a lefty against Mathewson, so he did see the ball trace off, which is why the fadeaway earned a somewhat contrary name.)

Happily, Mathewson's frame of mind, so battered by his own desultory experience with the dreadful Giants, improved when he went back to Bucknell after the '00 season. That was largely because it was then that he met Jane Stoughton. A Sunday school teacher who came from a prominently social Lewisburg family, Jane had been engaged to a fraternity brother of Mathewson's, but that romance had ended by the time she met the biggest man on campus. Soon Matty was courting her. His confidence, buoyed by love and by the acclaim for all his usual and sundry campus accomplishments, was such that he left Bucknell as a junior in March of oughty-one to go to spring training. He never went back to Bucknell to get his degree, although there is this, too: just as McGraw chose to return to Baltimore, his wife's hometown, to be buried, so would Mathewson be laid to rest in the place where first he came to fame, where first he met the love of his life.

FIVE

From 1903 to 1953, major league baseball went through a half century when not a single team in either league moved. Rule changes were minute. While no American institution was more reliable than baseball in the first half of the twentieth century, this incredible period of sustained stability was in direct contrast to what had preceded it (or, for that matter, what would follow). In the early decades of professional baseball, not only did franchises routinely come and go, but so did whole leagues. Because most ballparks were relatively cheap wooden structures, often jerry-built jumbles of kindling constructed by the owner, not the municipality, teams were not tied to their city in any substantive way. The rules were also changed regularly and dramatically as the proprietors sought to find the most attractive game that balanced offense and defense.

In 1892, for example, the National League batting average was .245 and plummeting, so a pitching rubber was stationed in the ground in order to anchor the pitcher, and the distance from the rubber to home plate was lengthened. At first it was proposed that the pitcher be stationed exactly halfway between home and second. This would have made the pitching distance sixty-three feet, six inches, eight feet longer than the established distance at that time.

This, however, was deemed too radical, so one of the poobahs idly suggested that they just add five feet to the existing standard. So was begat the curious distance of sixty feet, plus six inches — which is nowadays assumed to be a perfect measure, ordained by God Himself. Anyway, even designed by imperfect man, it worked. Strikeouts were cut in half in 1893, and the league batting average soared to .280.

A few years later, just as Mathewson entered the majors, the pitchers were thrown a bone to even things up more, when it was decided that, before two strikes, foul balls must count as strikes. Home plate itself was changed to its current configuration — rectangle at the top, triangle at the bottom — and enlarged, so that, at seventeen inches across, it presented a target one inch wider than it had been. In a very real way, Mathewson came to play at exactly the right time for a pitcher, just as, two decades later, Babe Ruth would profit as a slugger when the spitball was outlawed and the balls themselves were juiced up. Baseball statistics are not quite as pure as the mandarins of the game would have you believe. The various eras are distinctly different from one another. The 1890s, without foul strikes, equates very nicely to the recent years, with steroids.

But at least as radical as the rules changes was what happened to the very structure of the game. First, after the 1899 season, the National League — which had been the only major league for some time — rid itself of three of its weakest sisters: Louisville, Washington, and Cleveland. A fourth franchise had to go, and clearly it could not be New York, even if the Giants had been at the bottom of the standings along with the artless Colonels, Senators, and Spiders. Instead, even though Baltimore had finished quite respectfully in fourth place and succeeded at the box office, and was, too, barely removed from its legendary epoch, the Orioles got the death card.

The reason was that Baltimore, always a branch town, had sold out its franchise to

Brooklyn ownership before the start of the '99 season. Such was syndicate baseball. The Bridegrooms, after finishing a dismal tenth in '98, then simply plucked Ned Hanlon from Baltimore as its new manager, plus snared three twenty-game winners as well as Kelley, Keeler, Jennings, and "Big Dan" McGann, a slugging first baseman. Renamed the Superbas, Brooklyn then promptly jumped nine positions to win the '99 pennant. Among other things, this positively infuriated Andrew Freedman, who didn't think Brooklyn should even be allowed in the league any longer because, when Brooklyn lost its status as a city and was folded into New York as a borough in 1898, this meant that New York had two teams, and National League rules stipulated only one per city. But nobody took Freedman's whining seriously, and he began to scheme for the ultimate in syndicate baseball, wherein *all* the teams in the league would be owned by one cartel. Unable to pull that off, he became even more penurious, so that the team young Christy Mathewson would soon join grew all the more bereft of talent and unloved by the populace.

On the other hand, given what scraps their Brooklyn owners had left them, the

Orioles' fourth-place finish in '99 was extraordinary. Specifically, it was a spectacular achievement by the rookie twenty-six-year-old manager McGraw, whom Hanlon had tapped to succeed him. The Orioles actually gave the Superbas a run for their money right into August, even as McGraw's team was called The Leftovers, The Castoffs, or The Orphans. Tom Murphy, the groundskeeper, formed the name MCGRAW in white posies over by the Oriole bench, and Baltimore fans so took to McGraw's minions that the team actually made a slight profit in '99. Not only that, but such attractive scrappers were the Birds that they led the league in road attendance. But never mind. Even though Baltimore was the sixth-largest city in the nation, the syndicate folded the franchise so that the National League could be reduced to a more manageable eight clubs. So off went McGraw to St. Louis for the 1900 season, to pick up his ten thousand dollars in mad money and consider his long-term prospects.

And sure enough, soon enough, Ban Johnson came calling. He was ready to bring large eastern seaboard cities into his Western League, christen it the American League, and make it not only a big league challenge to the National, but decency's darling. Johnson's teams raided the established National League, and about seventy-five players jumped — or, rather, in the argot of the time, they "kangarooed out." Cleverly, Johnson had his invading troops steer pretty clear of Pittsburgh. That was the smallest city in the National League, so by allowing the strength of the league to flower by the Monongahela, it diminished interest in the franchises in the larger cities. Johnson was a smart cookie. The Pirates dominated the National League until McGraw was able to build up the Giants.

The ideal managerial model for the new league was the straitlaced Connie Mack, who took over the Philadelphia franchise. Mack looked to a relatively new source to stock his Athletics — colleges. Most particularly, he signed a farmer who had graduated from Gettysburg College, Eddie Plank, a left-handed pitcher who would become the mainstay of his staff. He also offered that fifteen hundred dollars to young Christy Mathewson, whom Freedman had dumped back into the tidewater, at Norfolk, and when Mathewson accepted the fifty-dollar advance, he tacitly became a Philadelphia Athletic.

Meanwhile, Ban Johnson was after McGraw to manage the new American League team that he wished to place in Baltimore. Obviously the profane McGraw did not fit into Johnson's template for a civil, upstanding, rather Victorian American League, but Johnson needed Baltimore, so Muggsy became a necessary evil. On November 12, 1900, Johnson arrived in Baltimore, dining there on considerable amounts of champagne and pheasant with McGraw and Wilbert Robinson, who were then duly awarded pieces of the franchise. The Baltimore Orioles were back in business, with John J. McGraw as manager. When the season opened with a parade, the Baltimore Shooting Association carried complementary banners that read: FAREWELL, NATIONAL LEAGUE SYNDICATE BASEBALL AND MERCENARY METHODS and WELCOME, AMERICAN LEAGUE, HONEST BALL, AND SPORTSMANLIKE METHODS.

Perhaps never before or since would Muggsy be so on the side of the angels. Ban Johnson himself threw out the first ball, McGraw was presented with a huge basket of roses, and, when he came to bat the first time, the grateful throng gave him a three-minute standing ovation. They knew it was Muggsy who had gotten Baltimore back into the bigs. He responded by belting a double off the right-field fence. Moreover, the whole American League was an instant success, drawing 1,683,000, only a couple hundred thousand less than the established National League — which has, ever since, been known in sportswriter argot as the "senior circuit."

Part of the reason for the American League's immediate success was that it seemed, well, more American. That is, the league's franchise antecedents were in the Middle West — where four of its teams were still located: Chicago, Milwaukee, Detroit, and Cleveland — and its players tended to appear to be more wholesome heartland Protestant farmboys compared with the National League's Irish Roman roustabouts. This genealogy played into Ban Johnson's claims of more genteel play.

Germans were by far the largest non-English-speaking group of immigrants in the U.S. at that time. They tended to move to the west and, notwithstanding the Teutonic warlike images we are all used to by now, the German-Americans were not fond of boxing. Rather, they took first to bowling, where their camaraderie, *gemütlichkeit,* and love of beer were best served together. Indeed, the way German immigrants bowled was to have *three* teams compete against each other. This way, on a rotating basis, while two bowled, one was always available to step up to the bar and guzzle suds.

But, like the Irish, the Germans also quickly took to the American national sport. St. Patrick's Day club games between German and Irish immigrants were common in many cities in the latter part of the nineteenth century. To the ire of the Irish, too, the Germans were much more graciously accepted by the established English-Americans. The German newcomers were not nearly so denigrated, even though a German accent was long a staple for vaudeville comics — the most famous being the Dr. Kronkheit character of Smith & Dale.

Baltimore itself was an eastern seaboard outpost for German immigrants, with two score breweries. (One of its main downtown thoroughfares was, in fact, German Street, although this would be changed to Redwood Street when the U.S. went to war with the Hun in 1917.) So the town was more than a good demographic match for the new American League. The Orioles drew 141,000 that inaugural season, which

76

was no great shakes, but the franchise lost only a little money. But then, the Orioles were a fairly ordinary team, and they were bedeviled by injuries. McGraw, in fact, was credited with a superb job in guiding such a nondescript crew home to a slightly better than .500 finish. His personal reputation as a manager only grew. He also batted .349 himself, even though he was effectively finished as a regular ballplayer in August when he reinjured a bad knee. He would come to bat only 195 more times in his career.

Worse, though, Muggsy began to butt heads with Ban Johnson on a regular basis. His best hitter was a handsome devil named "Turkey Mike" Donlin, who had kangarooed out of St. Louis, where he had been a teammate of McGraw's the year before. Turkey Mike — so called because, it was said, he could strut even while sitting down — was simply irremedial, and was in the middle of a melee on August 21 that escalated into a full-scale riot in a game against Detroit. Although McGraw, who was nearly lame at the time, stayed at the side of the umpire, Tommy Connolly, protecting him from the marauding crowd that Donlin had incited, Muggsy's star pitcher, "Iron Man" McGinnity, had already stomped on Connolly's feet and twice unleashed great rivers of tobacco juice into the ump's face. Connolly forfeited the game to Detroit, and then Johnson barred McGinnity for life.

McGraw, overruling his own doctors, who had told him to keep his knee immobilized, went to Chicago, petitioning Johnson personally, and the two men momentarily buried the hatchet. McGinnity apologized and was reinstated, but if it was a brief lifetime suspension for him, it was also no more than a temporary armistice between Johnson and McGraw. President Johnson had surely already decided that the American League would profit with both McGraw and Baltimore jettisoned. It was only a matter of time.

In this lawless interlude for baseball, Mathewson, meanwhile, had found his way back to the Giants. When Freedman discovered that the collegian had kangarooed out to the Athletics, he threatened Mathewson with banishment from the game, and the kid, unsure of his position, even as several all-stars jumped to the new league, decided he better stick with New York. He felt terrible about taking Connie Mack's fifty bucks bonus, though, and made Freedman promise he would repay the Philadelphia manager. Only years later did Mathewson discover that Freedman had reneged, so then he sent Mr. Mack the money.

Freedman, of course, had no idea what a prize he had salvaged. Mathewson's return to the Giants in '01 was a complete turnaround. The debutante who had been hit hard in every appearance the year before was suddenly the ace of the staff. He won his first game against the Superbas 5–3, allowing only four hits and two walks while striking out eight. It was a tough setting for young Mathewson, too, for it was the home opener, with a huge turnout of ninety-eight hundred. "It was the same old baseball crowd," the *Times* reported, "never behind with its advice and always ready to applaud a good play." The Catholic prefectory band played, and the fire commissioner threw out the first ball. The Superbas were sure they could rattle the college boy, but midway through the game, Ned Hanlon told his troops to put a cork in it. It was obvious that rather than upsetting him, Mathewson was feeding off the razzing. Somehow, Matty had tamed his freak pitch and grown up, both, overnight.

At this time the favored verb to describe what pitchers did was "officiate." Well,

this day Christy Mathewson really officiated for the first time. He won his next
seven decisions, too, and on July 15 he officiated a no-hitter against St. Louis. No-
hitters were so rare that their unique
quality really wasn't yet appreciated. "The
collegian let Donovan's men down
without a hit," was how the *Sun* summed
things up, blandly. The *Times* didn't even
get it, merely referring to his "excellent
pitching."

Mathewson was so much better than
anybody could have imagined that Andrew Freedman actually gave him two
suits in midseason as a bonus.
Mathewson's record tailed off somewhat
as the dismal Giant season wore along,
but that was more a function of the fail-
ures of the whole rotten team than it was
of him, officiating. He finished all but two
of the thirty-eight games he started,
throwing five shutouts and posting a 2.41
earned run average. On a team that won a
mere fifty-two games, Mathewson won
twenty (losing seventeen).

Meanwhile, in Baltimore, as this season
of 1901 wore down and McGraw limped
around on his bum leg, he heard plenty
about the Giants' young star in the other
league. Maybe he even remembered get-

ting a hit off him in St. Louis the previous year. Muggsy didn't forget much, and he especially liked tall pitchers and college men.

At this time, the nation suffered a great tragedy, though. President William McKinley was assassinated in Buffalo, and on September 14, 1901 (September '01s are ominous months for the U.S.), Theodore Roosevelt, the only president ever born in New York City, was inaugurated. It was barely three years since he had had his uniform custom-made at Brooks Brothers and gaily gone off to charge up San Juan Hill in Cuba. Now there were already genial reports of the soldiers halfway round the world, in the Philippines, teaching naked natives how to play the American national sport.

The United States had become something of an empire despite itself, and New York was surely the hub of this strange new indefinable international conglomerate. The buildings kept flying up, higher, and the immigrants kept pouring in. And, whatever his affection for Baltimore, it was apparent that Muggsy had outgrown the Monumental City and the Diamond Café. In fact, in many respects he was more the Little Teddy than he was the Little Napoleon. Among other things, they had both lost a young wife. But the tragedies in Muggsy's life were, finally, mostly behind him.

By contrast, Matty's all lay ahead.

SIX

One of the few loyal Giant fans was a long-faced thespian named DeWolf Hopper. He loved baseball no less than marriage, for he was a regular at the Polo Grounds and five times entered into the estate of holy matrimony — on the last occasion with a struggling young actress less than half his age who took his name. That was Hedda Hopper, who became more famous as a Hollywood gossip columnist. Anyway, long before that development, DeWolf Hopper had begun reciting a poem. He started almost immediately after it had originally appeared in print, in the *San Francisco Examiner* of June 3, 1888. He orated it first at Wallack's Theatre in New York and never stopped, wherever he was. "How many times can best be numbered by the stars in the Milky Way," he opined in 1924.

The poem, of course, was "Casey at the Bat," which, most appropriately, was subtitled "A Ballad of the Republic." It was written by a young Harvard man named Ernest Thayer, who never wrote anything else of any consequence in his life. "Casey at the Bat" is generally considered to be the best-known American poem, ahead of Joyce Kilmer's "Trees."

Unlike Thayer, who was a genuine crank, Jack Norworth, author of "Harvest Moon" and "Meet Me at Apple Blossom Time," had never so much as seen a baseball game when, one fine day in 1908, while riding on a train into New York, he glanced out the window and saw a sign that read: base ball today — polo grounds.

Immediately, Norworth dashed off four stanzas of "Take Me Out to the Ball Game" and carried them down to Tin Pan Alley, where he found a musician, Albert Von Tilzer, who had likewise never seen a baseball game, and had him scribble out a tune. After the National Anthem, other patriotic hymns, and "Happy Birthday," "Take Me Out to the Ball Game" is probably the most familiar American song that there is.

Curiously, the great American baseball poem and the great American baseball song share two things. First, both feature a Casey. There is mighty Casey (he was given no first name) who strode to the plate (and to his sad, tragic destiny) with ease in his manner, and then there is Katie Casey, who is identified as the young lady who wishes to be escorted to the park, there to enjoy the crowd and partake of peanuts and Cracker Jack. Second, the poem and the song both have a negative ending. Not a home run, not even, mind you, a scratch single. But no: the worst. Mighty Casey strikes out, just as Katie Casey, who is baseball mad, knows that there are "one, two, three strikes you're out at the old ball game."

Perhaps this is not so odd. As baseball apostles are forever fond of pointing out, even the best hitters make out two out of every three times. For all the sappy references about how perfect a game baseball was for America, maybe the fact that it was simply so hard to succeed at was its most salient appeal. Following that, perhaps it has always been easier for the pitchers, even the worst of whom get most batters out, to see the game more benignly than the batters.

Anyway, Christy Mathewson said: "Baseball is always played out in the sunshine, where the air is pure and the grass is green, and there is something about the game . . . which teaches one to win or lose as a gentleman should, and that is a very fine thing to learn."

While John McGraw said: "In playing or managing, the game of ball is only fun for me when I'm out front and winning. I don't give a hill of beans for the rest of the game. The man who loses gracefully loses easily. Sportsmanship and easygoing methods are all right, but . . . once a team of mine is on the diamond, I want it to fight. Namby-pamby methods don't get much in results."

In any event, as 1902 began, both McGraw and Mathewson were caught up in wretched seasons that would, soon enough, bring these two opposite characters together. First: poor young Matty. Impossible as it might seem, the Giants descended to yet another lower rung, posting the very worst record in either league. Manager George Davis had escaped Freedman, jumping to the Chicago White Stockings. In his stead, Freedman chose a former Philadelphia sportswriter, Horace Fogel, but the second baseman, Heinie Smith, had the ear of many of his teammates. It was chaos, and the newspapers were merciless. The Giants were now called "positively the rankest apology for a first-class ballclub that was ever imposed upon any major city."

The team itself was riven along Protestant-Catholic lines, which was then closer to a Sunni-Shiite breach than what passes for division in Christianity today. Fueled by an organization known as the American Protective Association, there remained a great deal of anti–Roman Catholic sentiment in the land, and the Irish on the team were naturally defensive about prejudice, real or perceived. It reveals a lot about religious feelings at that time to know that after his success in Manila Bay — "You may fire when ready, Gridley!" — Adm. George Dewey was the most admired man in America; however, when he, a widower, married a woman who had been raised Protestant but turned Catholic, then did he instantly fall out of favor with much of mainstream America.

Religion aside, the Giants were just a generally unattractive lot. Mrs. McGraw would call them "ne'er-do-wells, knockers, shirkers and loafers." Mathewson, the young sportsman, was at sea in their company. After his spectacular 1901, he had gotten a substantial raise to thirty-five hundred dollars, but despite pitching a shutout before an overflow crowd in the opener, he couldn't duplicate his previous year's success. As the season wore on, some of the more jealous Giants turned on him. When the clueless erstwhile scribe, Fogel, was relieved of his managerial scepter in June, Heinie Smith took formal command, whereupon some of the regulars prevailed on the new manager to remove Mathewson from the rotation and play him in the field. Stationed at first base then, they would purposely make bad throws to him, in the dirt, off the bag. Soon the finest hurler of his generation was actually being referred to in the press as, "Christy Mathewson, the former pitcher."

Meanwhile, McGraw's situation in Baltimore was hardly better. Before the 1902 season even began, Turkey Mike Donlin, loaded to the gills, slugged a showgirl's escort, and then when she pleaded, "Please don't hit him," Turkey Mike popped her too. He was arrested, tried, and imprisoned — and, over McGraw's protests, he was also released by the Orioles. Such ungentlemanly behavior was not the image Ban Johnson had in mind for his league's players. Furthermore, he ordered the umpires to put the screws to Muggsy. Soon McGraw was complaining that even if an opponent merely claimed that he was being held by the belt at third, the umpire would wave him home. Rumors began to heat up that McGraw simply couldn't survive under Johnson's thumb and would have to take leave of the decency-encrusted American League. Johnson fanned the flames by saying that McGraw would be traitorous if he deserted Baltimore, and, with his dander up, the Little Napoleon replied with a wonderful historical mix-and-match. "So, the Julius Caesar of the league calls me a Benedict Arnold, does he?" Muggsy harumphed.

Then in late May things came to a boil when McGraw was spiked in a game against Detroit, suffering a three-inch gash below his left knee. In a rage, Muggsy attacked the Tiger who had injured him, smashing his jaw, before being carried off the field. McGraw's innocent bride looked on in shock. "It was the first outburst of his rage that I had seen, and it wasn't easy to watch," she recalled. It must have been a horribly bloody scene. Johnson suspended Muggsy for five days.

The next shoe dropped on June 28 in a game against Boston, which was being umpired by McGraw's special bête noire, Tommy Connolly. After arguing with Connolly, who was standing between first and second, McGraw started back to the bench. He paused and, according to McGraw, only screamed back a warning: "Connolly, you'd better get out of the line. Somebody will jump you and spike you." Maybe McGraw had somewhat embellished these remarks; maybe Connolly thought there was sufficient threat inherent within them. Whatever, he tossed McGraw out of the game.

Muggsy was livid. "I used no expletives. Nor did I do anything that would warrant my being sent to the clubhouse, yet Connolly, in a most insulting way, ordered me off the field," he explained. "I made up my mind right there that I would no longer stand for being made a dog and refused to go." So when McGraw continued to resist departing the diamond, Connolly forfeited the game. Accordingly, two days later, Johnson suspended him again, whereupon McGraw hastened to New York and began secret discussions with Andrew Freedman. Publicly he called the American League "a loser," Ban Johnson "a czar," and, for good measure, he disparaged Connie Mack's Athletics as "white elephants."

As Muggsy's New York negotiations began to leak out, McGraw (still in his woe-is-me canine stage) lashed out even more at Johnson, saying: "I would be a fool to stay here and have a dog made of myself by a man who makes no pretense of investigating or giving a hearing to both sides."

Johnson replied with contempt, even denying McGraw animal status. "The muttering of an insignificant and vindictive wasp," he snorted.

That did it. McGraw was gone from Baltimore. He had loaned the Oriole franchise seven thousand dollars, and so he demanded that he either be reimbursed or released. "I acted fast," he explained. "Someone would be left holding the bag, and I made up my mind that it wouldn't be me. I simply protected myself as any business-man would." And, most emphatically: "I did not jump." That was very important to him. He maintained that position all his life. Even long after he died, his wife continued to argue that her husband had done nothing wrong in departing her Baltimore. "Baseball . . . is a business. It is a man's world," she wrote. "Perhaps a mother's savage defense of her brood might be likened to a man's battle to salvage wealth, position, power or whatever was in jeopardy at the time."

McGraw himself also publicly declared: "I wish to assure Baltimore that in consideration of their kindness, I shall not tamper with any of the Baltimore Club's players. I would not do that, because of my friendship for the people here, and because it would not be right."

Then, promptly, he took four players — including Iron Man McGinnity — with him to New York, so eviscerating the franchise that Baltimore had to forfeit a game. Good grief, he even seduced Tom Murphy, the canny groundskeeper, into taking his gardening magic to the Polo Grounds. The *New York Sun* flatly called the Giants "the Baltimorized New Yorks." The *Sporting News* was no less distracted by McGraw's claims, characterizing him as "the Aguinaldo of base ball." Since Aguinaldo was a Filipino rebel who had been a special thorn in the American army's side, that was pretty harsh stuff, in the modern range of naming someone the "Osama bin Laden of baseball."

Meanwhile, back in Mobtown, Ban Johnson invoked league rules and gleefully took over the Oriole franchise, which is what he had wanted to do all along. By next season, 1903, he would have a whole team of Baltimorized New Yorks in his own league. They would be called the Highlanders at first, but would become somewhat better known under their subsequent sobriquet, the Yankees.

McGraw and Johnson never exchanged another word as long as they lived.

The Giants were on a western swing when McGraw officially took over the club on July 17. He accepted an $11,000 contract, the highest in the sport to that time, topping his own record $10,000 salary with St. Louis. Promptly he cleaned house, cutting loose nine of the team's twenty-three players. Freedman was apoplectic, since this meant having to eat $14,000 in salaries, but he had signed over authority to McGraw, and Muggsy unabashedly took charge. If there had been any doubt on Freedman's part, this probably sealed his decision to get out of the baseball business. Tammany had been kicked out of power in the previous November's election, and Freedman realized that he no longer possessed the authority to prohibit the construction of a new ballpark, which had previously been a key factor in keeping the American League out of New York. It was bad enough that Brooklyn had a franchise to rival his Giants, but now another competitor loomed in Manhattan.

The team was just as shook up at

McGraw's hovering presence as was the owner. "The New-Yorks are suffering from nervousness in anticipation of the coming of manager McGraw," wrote the *World*'s baseball reporter. "It is said that some of the men are dissipating, which accounts for the miserable play of the team."

Mathewson himself was back at the pitcher's rubber, having played his last game at first base on July 1, but when Muggsy's purge began, a rumor started flying that McGraw was going to offload Matty to St. Louis. Wrote the *Tribune*: "It is said that Mathewson, the pitcher [at least he was no longer 'the former pitcher'], may be allowed to go, as it is believed that he and McGraw are not on the best of terms." Matty allowed as how that was all news to him, but given the two men's contrasting personalities, it is certainly understandable that there was an assumption that he couldn't tolerate his new manager. As for McGraw, he never so much as contemplated getting rid of Mathewson. On the contrary, he called Matty's brief exile from pitching "sheer insanity," adding that "any man who did that should be locked up."

And then the Baltimorized Giants returned from their western road swing to

the Polo Grounds, and, essentially, baseball began for real in the Borough of
Manhattan, City of New York. For his first
game as Giants' manager on Saturday, July
19, 1902, McGraw started the redoubtable
McGinnity. After a succession of handfuls
for crowds, suddenly a throng of sixteen
thousand materialized, almost filling the
park. McGraw placed himself at shortstop
and went one-for-three. "It is impossible
for the aggressive little baseball expert to
keep out of the game," the *Times* noted,
and the other papers, which had been lac-
erating the Giants for years, suddenly were
in his thrall. Even though the Giants lost
4–3, there was, it seems, overnight, a whole
new spirit discernible from the press box.
"The old-time Baltimore ginger infused by
McGraw held out to the end," the *World*
cheered. The other hard-boiled diamond
journalists joined the joyful chorus.

McGraw always understood how to work
the press. Sports pages had begun to
flourish back in the 1880s shortly before
McGraw came into the game, and so he
sort of grew up with them. He knew how
to reel out just enough of the skinny to
convince the writers that they were his
confidants; also, he trusted them with se-
lected inside tidbits. "I have never known a

baseball reporter to violate a secret," he declared near the end of his career. Indeed, one time in spring training, when his irresponsible pitcher Bugs Raymond appeared to have broken his promise and fallen off the water wagon, McGraw convened a secret jury of writers to deliver a verdict on the matter. They did. They adjudged Raymond guilty but, co-opted by being inducted into the Giants' judicial process, none of them wrote a word about Bugs's fall from grace.

Before McGraw came to New York, of course, Freedman had made sure that the Giants endured the worst possible press from the score or so papers in town. Worse, the Giants could be almost ignored. At that time, when athletic professionalism was still not altogether accepted, it was not uncommon for the papers to devote almost as much space to college baseball games as to the pros. College football was heavily reported in the autumn, although on a regular basis, horse racing got the biggest play of all; in the upscale broadsheets, there was also extended coverage of regattas. The new sport of auto racing spilled over into both the society pages, to report on the swells in attendance, and the news pages, where speed and death (or the threat thereof) has always commanded a broad audience. But major league baseball was a staple, even if the coverage was often captious and dismissive, and usually written in so rococo a style that, looking back, the critic Jonathan Yardley observed: "The sports pages seemed to be a bad dream by Sir Walter Scott."

The newspaper custom bothered to identify the players only by their last names. By the same token, the writers themselves were almost never given bylines. (The most famous was Bat Masterson, the old gunslinger, who had decamped to New York earlier in '02, having hung up his six-shooters to become both a deputy U.S. marshal, as appointed by Teddy Roosevelt, and a sports columnist with the *Morning Telegram*. Masterson's sports specialty was boxing, though.)

In the event, as soon as McGraw came to town, the Giants were accorded much greater and more enthusiastic coverage. After all, McGraw was, simply, news. Mathewson, as we shall see, was not so much news as he was a reliable feature, like the weather or the comic strips. He could do no wrong. As newspapers began to use players' first names, many of them, even as commonplace as "Jack," say, or

"Bill," would be referred to, like that, in quotation marks. Mathewson's never was so adorned. It was almost as if "Matty" was a title. Here, for example, is a newspaper photo caption of the Giants' 1913 starters: "Tesreau, Matty, Marquard and Demaree." And when Matty won, as he usually did, this was proof again that some good things you could count on — even in dog-eat-dog Noo Yawk. If Matty lost, it was an aberration that must be explained, invariably chalked up to bum luck or poor hitting or fielding by his ungrateful teammates. But somehow, Matty wasn't really news in the conventional sense. He was just Matty.

It was the custom at that time for major league teams to employ many of their off days picking up extra money playing local sandlot nines, and so it was that when McGraw first took over the Giants and sent Mathewson to the pitcher's box it was, of all things, against the Orange Athletic Club, over in New Jersey. That was July 22. Matty gave up a run to the amateurs in the very first inning, too, and while it is unclear how long McGraw used him, the Giants eventually prevailed 3–2, and McGraw was satisfied enough to give Matty a start two days later in Brooklyn.

That was the real beginning of their beautiful friendship, as Mathewson shut out the home team 2–0 on a five-hitter. The *Sun* even proclaimed that "it was the most perplexing pitching snag the Brooklynites have struck this season." Not only that, but now the *World* lauded the erstwhile sluggish Giants as "McGraw's hustlers."

However, as nice as any victory and the team's shiny new image was, McGraw had already written off 1902. He spent much of the balance of the season away from the team, scouting prospects and trade bait for 1903. The team managed to win only forty-eight games, finishing fifty-three and a half games behind the Pirates. Mathewson led the staff with fourteen victories, and although he lost seventeen games, he pitched eight shutouts and posted an earned run average of 2.11. On his off days, closely monitoring Iron Man McGinnity when he pitched, Matty even picked up a much better change-up. It would be another thirteen years before Mathewson would win less than twenty games or lose more games than he won in a season. Anyway, he was going home to Pennsylvania with hopes of convincing Jane to become his wife.

As for McGraw, he was especially

pleased that, at the end of the season, John Brush, "the Hoosier Wanamaker," unloaded his controlling interest in the Cincinnati Reds and bought the Giants from Freedman. Brush was a semi-invalid who walked with a cane, suffering as he was from rheumatism and some disease of the nervous system (that possibly had been caused by syphilis). He was not the easiest of men, but, of course, compared to Freedman he was a dreamboat. McGraw adored him. The fact that Brush despised Ban Johnson and his renegade American League only marginally less than did Muggsy bound the two men together stronger than any hoops of steel ever could. Ironically, it was Brush who had sought "purification" on the field a few years earlier, but now that he and McGraw were on the same team, he accommodated himself to Muggsy's rude antics. The only McGravian behavorial flaw that Brush never seems to have been able to turn a blind eye to was the manager's penchant for going out to the track and playing a few races before heading to the Polo Grounds for games that usually started at three-thirty or four.

McGraw was even a partner of Brush's of a sort, for when Freedman unloaded the team, Mrs. McGraw had purchased four shares of the Giants at $250 apiece. The McGraws were now happily partaking of New York nightlife. They were ensconced in a suite at the Victoria Hotel at Fifth Avenue and Twenty-seventh Street, so high up they could barely hear the *cloppety-clop* of the horse-drawn carriages that still plied the street. Instead, the McGraws might hear the *putt-putt* sounds of the newfangled "devil wagons" that came to be called cars, or the grand new twenty-four-passenger double-decker buses that the Fifth Avenue Coach Company had started to run.

From the vantage of their parlor, though, the McGraws could watch the construction of a spectacular new skyscraper, the Flatiron Building, rising twenty-one stories toward the heavens down on Twenty-third Street. On the street there, the sharpies would lollygag about outside the Flatiron, leering at the women walking by. There was plenty of opportunity. A third of the clerical workers in New York were now female; why, nineteenth-century shopgirls had become twentieth-century saleswomen. What the guys standing on the corner of Twenty-third and Broadway were waiting for were the by-products of the downdrafts common to the area. With a good gust, one that would blow up a skirt enough to reveal bare ankles, the fellas would all call out: "Twenty-three skidoo!"

McGraw might not have approved. Curiously, he was always very old-fashioned, even somewhat puritanical, when it came to the fairer sex. Now, of course, his own better half, like most respectable women, was still in long skirts — their hems invariably dirtied as they walked the sidewalks of New York. After all, sanitation workers still had to deal with thousands of gallons of horse urine and thousands of tons of horse manure every day, East Side, West Side, all around town.

But things were beginning to change. With the new century, skirts that didn't reach quite all the way to the ground, called "rainy-daisies," were starting to be accepted in fast company. Women were taking to exercise, riding the newfangled bicycles. "Daisy, Daisy, give me your answer true . . ." And out in Brooklyn, Coney Island had a roller coaster and a Ferris wheel and new amusement parks, and the beaches were thronged with women of all shapes and sizes in the newest risqué bathing costumes. Richard K. Fox, editor of the *Police Gazette*, the popular men's journal that thrived on three attractions —

crime, sex, and boxing — offered this observation: "If a man is troubled with illusions concerning the female form divine, and wishes to be rid of those illusions, he should go to Coney Island and closely watch the thousands of women who bathe there every Sunday."

Sunday baseball in New York, however, was still considered a sinful temptation for the workingman and would not be allowed for many more years. Matty's mother, Minerva, certainly subscribed to that view, and Matty listened to his mother.

SEVEN

So Fatso Ban Johnson got his wish. For the 1903 season he moved the Orioles to New York, thus, it turned out, setting the major leagues in stone with the same sixteen franchises for the next fifty years. Oh, with time a few nicknames would change, RIP: the Beaneaters, Superbas, Orphans, Perfectos, Terrors, Blues, and Highlanders. The latter earned their name because, with Tammany out of power, the American League was finally able to find a place to build a stadium — only the lone option was on the highest ground on Manhattan Island, in Washington Heights, in the far upper reaches of the borough. There was Hilltop Park, a simple wooden structure seating sixteen thousand, raised. It was pretty easy to fling up stadiums in those days (it was also pretty easy for them to either fall down or burn down).

What would become the New York Yankees franchise was purchased for eighteen thousand dollars, the new owners being William Devery, a corrupt former police commissioner, and Frank Farrell, who was known as "the poolroom czar." Johnson was always ethically selective in putting his wholesome new league together.

McGraw eliminated the American League from his mind, content to enjoy the delights of the big city, build up the Giants' roster, and prepare to take his first New York team to spring training in Savannah. Mathewson had an even more memorable spring training, for it was his honeymoon. He and Jane were married at her parents' home in Lewisburg on March 5. The bride's family approved of Matty and liked him immensely, even if her father was dubious that his new son-in-law should attempt to "make a living playing a child's sport with a bunch of uneducated ruffians."

But the wedding was the highlight of the Lewisburg social calendar, and immediately after the fancy reception, the bride and groom caught the Buffalo Flyer south as Matty's smirking groomsmen handed out leaflets at the depot, advertising the presence of the newlyweds on their wedding night. "He will be easily recognized by his boyish countenance and Apollo-like form," the pamphlets advised the other wayfarers.

Before plighting their troth, though, Jane and Matty had agreed to something of a pre-nup. In the even-up deal, he consented to leave his Baptist upbringing and worship in Jane's Presbyterian church while, in return, she swore to give up her Democratic affiliation and join his Republican Party. Bully.

In Savannah, Jane was a notable figure at the De Soto Hotel, for it was unusual for players to bring their wives along. At some point another woman spied her there in the lobby, sizing her up cattily even if she would later write that it was "*not* a catty reaction." And John McGraw did *not* do dirt to Baltimore. The observer was Blanche McGraw, Muggsy's wife of a year, who was Baltimore Catholic nouveau. Blanche found the Protestant country girl too "strait-laced . . . a Sunday-school teacher, which also made her suspect." Not only that, but Blanche didn't care for the way that Jane was sneaking peeks back at her. She was certain that Jane, unadorned as she was pretty, was looking down on her for her sequins and jewelry, that she must be thinking that Blanche was a "hussy."

Nevertheless Blanche grew curious, and

although she decided that she could not ask him about the bride herself, she did finally bring herself to casually inquire of Muggsy about the newlywed young right-hander. "Looks like he can pitch with his head as well as his arm," he replied.

Of course, Blanche didn't mean that. She didn't mean *baseball*. She wanted to find out what sort of a fellow the lovely brunette's husband was. But she should have known what sort of an answer to expect. This was how Blanche assessed her husband: "Life without baseball had very little meaning to him. It was his meat, drink, dream, his blood and breath, his very reason for existence." So it fell to Blanche McGraw to approach Jane Mathewson, and one day soon thereafter in the lobby of the De Soto, she ventured to introduce herself.

Although there might not have been as much apparent difference between the two wives as between the two husbands, there did not, either, appear to be much common ground between the two women. But, in fact, they hit it off right away, and while the men practiced their craft at Forsyth Park, the women chatted and laughed, took tea together, and wandered about Savannah, shopping and sight-seeing, enjoying the warm Dixie air. By the time the Giants prepared to head north, Blanche and Jane not only were friends, but they had brought their husbands closer together.

Matty, of course, had always admired Muggsy. Now he grew to like him. Muggsy liked Matty, too. Of course, everybody did. McGraw must have been jealous of the tall and handsome and popular Mathewson. Of course, everybody else always was. But Muggsy also was impressed by Mathewson's sharp mind. McGraw, the high school dropout, could, slyly, often be more taken with a player's brain than with his talent. Blanche, though, also respected Mathewson's intellect. "He had an unusual mind, a quick mind, and the stubbornness of a person with a trained mind," she would say.

Muggsy was now thirty years old, almost eight years older than Mathewson. In baseball years, this was a lifetime. Not only that, but McGraw was an old thirty. As a matter of fact, his career as an active player was altogether ended here, one day in Savannah, when his right knee buckled on him during a workout. McGraw was odd; he never seemed to have had any in-between, going almost overnight from being a beardless Katzenjammer Kid to a paunchy dead ringer for W. C. Fields. By 1903 he'd already done some considerable living, too. Mathewson, by comparison, was downright callow. He was polite, McGraw pugnacious; Protestant to his Catholic; a country mouse to the city slicker Muggsy had become; pitcher to his batter; player to his manager; tall to his short; sportsman to his mucker. There seemed to be absolutely nothing that would match John J. McGraw with Christopher Mathewson.

But notwithstanding, so it was that before they returned north, the two couples agreed to live together back in New York. The four of them rented a ground-floor apartment for fifty dollars a month on the Upper West Side, at Columbus and Eighty-fifth Street, convenient to an el station on the line to the Polo Grounds. The way they worked it out was, Muggsy paid for the rent and the gas, and Matty paid for the food.

The arrangement turned out just fine, too. Blanche explained: "Jane and I led normal lives. We fed the men and left them alone to talk their baseball. Their happiness was our cause." Soon the two men made some financial investments together, too. This odd quartet — did ever any other manager and star player in any sport room together with their wives? — grew even closer in companionship and trust.

And always, McGraw and Mathewson talked the game of baseball. This was years before pitching coaches came into the sport, so even though Muggsy had never been a pitcher, Mathewson listened to him about his craft. It was also true that McGraw was not unintelligent on the subject. (In counterpoint, one recalls Jim Palmer telling his manager, the latter-day McGraw, Earl Weaver: "Earl, all you know about pitching is that you could never hit it.") When McGraw had first started playing baseball, as a child, he had been a pitcher. In fact, one time, when he was a candy butcher on a railroad and two passengers got into an argument about whether a baseball could truly curve, little Muggsy entered the discussion on behalf of the pro-curve gentleman. When the two riders struck a ten-dollar bet, the conductor bade the engineer stop the train. The passengers disembarked, and there, in a field by the side of the tracks, young McGraw found two stakes and set them up. He was never without a baseball, and so he stood back and pitched his ball, demonstratively swerving it around the stakes. Also, before the assembled returned to the train, for his effort he demanded and received one of the ten dollars that the winner of the bet had taken.

"Pitching was my first love," McGraw wrote in his memoirs. "To me, it is the most fascinating art in the world. It really is an art, too — not merely science." While he gave tips on technique to Mathewson — at this time, in 1903, for example, helping him improve the change-up he had picked up from Iron Man McGinnity — where he and Matty had their meeting of their minds was in that art of pitching. Location — the placement of pitches. And: mixing 'em up.

McGraw was amazed at how advanced a strategist young Mathewson was. Always there have been big, strong kids who are fireballers, capable of just flinging the horsehide past batters — and so too Mathewson. But almost from the start, Matty was also a thinking pitcher. In this one obvious way, the two different men were twinned. While McGraw called most pitches from the bench, early on he began to allow Mathewson the privilege of choosing his own pitches. Why, soon Muggsy paid him the ultimate compliment, actually comparing Matty to him-self. "It is rare," he humbly declared, "that a man like Christy Mathewson comes along who could remember like me."

That 1903 season would be magnificent for the Giants. McGraw took the worst team in the majors and added thirty-six victories. Only Pittsburgh and the Boston team in the American League posted better records. Just like that, too, the Giants became fashionable, the talk of the town. Crowds of up to thirty thousand began to show up for the biggest games, with hundreds — thousands? — more who would scamper up to watch from Coogan's Bluff, which overlooked the park (even if the choicest positions up there allowed but a limited vantage of the diamond).

Matty won thirty games while McGinnity won thirty-one. They were the first two pitchers since the National League got rid of its weak sisters and went with eight competitive clubs to win thirty. Three times that year McGinnity won dou-bleheaders, and he threw 434 innings, but as indefatigable as he was, curiously, the Iron Man had not earned his moniker for his endurance. Rather, before Muggsy dis-covered him and brought him to Baltimore in '99 at the advanced baseball age of twenty-eight, McGinnity had toiled at an iron foundry in Oklahoma.

If Iron Man won one more game than Matty, though, the younger man had, overall, a more impressive record. McGinnity lost twenty games, Mathewson only thirteen. Mathewson also had a slightly better earned run average — 2.26 to 2.43 — and a much better strikeout-to-walks ratio. Mathewson fanned 267 batters in 366 innings, to lead the league. Already he was the big favorite with the New York cranks — and he knew it, too. Like McGraw, he had a great sense of awareness; unlike McGraw, he had a sense of proportion to match. For all Mathewson's becoming modesty, he always understood how good he was — and how popular. McGraw's biographer, Charles C. Alexander, wrote that Matty was "an aloof, rather swell-headed young man, fully cognizant that he was the big attraction." Indeed, that he could hold himself apart from the hurly-burly might have made him appear somewhat stuck-up, but in time that very quality took on another perception, that he was indeed a special character and not one of the crowd.

Rube Marquard, a Hall of Famer himself, who would assume Iron Joe

McGinnity's role as the number two Giant pitcher, summed up his teammate this way: "Matty never thought he was better than anybody else. It was just the way he carried himself. . . . But it was okay because, what the hell, when you came to it, Matty *was* different."

Now, in 1903, happily married, secure with his manager and a winning team, Mathewson was definitely already beginning to develop into what he would become soon enough: the first real full-blooded American sports idol. Indeed, even by now, after just one season with McGraw's hustlers, Mathewson was well on his way to canonization. Perhaps at this point, only one other American athlete exceeded his popularity. And that wasn't even a human being; it was a horse: the great Dan Patch.

He was a light bay who stood more than sixteen and a half hands, with a heart that, in death, was revealed to be twice the size of a normal standardbred's. On October 12, 1903, Dan Patch paced a mile in 1:56½ seconds, a figure that would seem as astounding to savvy horse-conscious Americans at that time as sixty home runs would to baseball fans a generation later. Dan Patch traveled in his own private railway car and would routinely draw thirty to forty thousand fans when he raced. He would nod to his many fans and pose for cameras, and he was a marketing bonanza. The Dan Patch name was attached to watches, padlocks, sleds, and collars — even stoves and automobiles. There was even a dance named after him: the Dan Patch two-step. He was beloved of Americans. Only Matty would surpass him.

Although the Giants posted this spectacular turnaround success in 1903, and all credit fairly went to McGraw, he suffered a terrible personal setback early in the season. The Giants' number three starter was a deaf-mute named Dummy Taylor. In these more blunt times, where language was not so (as we say now) appropriate, all deaf-mutes in baseball were immediately tabbed Dummy (just as all Native Americans automatically became "Chief"). In one of the strangest of all baseball coincidences, in 1901, Mathewson's first full season in the majors, the Giants actually had three deaf-mutes on their pitching staff — George Leitner, Billy Deegan, and Taylor. All, naturally, were called Dummy. By '03 only Taylor remained in New York;

he was a fine pitcher. Also, since McGraw was never one to miss an opportunity, he liked having Taylor around on the bench when he wasn't starting in order that he might holler at the opponent's pitcher. Dummy Taylor emitted some kind of rattling shriek that could, apparently, be considerably disconcerting if you were about to deliver a pitch.

Taylor was in the outfield at the Polo Grounds, shagging flies, before the third game of the 1903 season. McGraw was near home plate, slapping grounders to his infielders. Taylor threw a ball back to the diamond that slammed into McGraw's face. He never saw it coming and went down as if he had been shot. The ball broke McGraw's nose, severing cartilage, and it also ruptured a blood vessel inside his throat. That caused the most incredible flood, the blood spurting out of both his nose and his mouth. Poor Dummy Taylor was beside himself while the other Giants looked on in shock at their fallen leader. McGraw was rushed to a hospital, where his nose was stuffed with cotton. At last the bleeding was stemmed, and he actually returned to the Polo Grounds late in the game.

The hemorrhaging soon returned, however. Indeed, the blow would affect McGraw's sinuses and cause debilitating upper respiratory infections for the rest of his life. But at that moment the Giants were scheduled to begin a road trip in Philadelphia, and, naturally, Muggsy prepared to leave town with his team. Blanche, however, put her foot down, telling her husband that she would not let him go unless she accompanied him. Reluctantly, McGraw finally agreed, but with one proviso: Matty must stay behind in New York. McGraw's reasoning was simply that he felt concern for Jane Mathewson, that, with Blanche in Philadelphia, she would be left alone in their large, new apartment in the strange, big city. McGraw mandated that Matty must stay with his young bride even though it meant that his star pitcher would miss his turn to start in Philadelphia.

Nobody had ever before heard of such a concession on the diamond from the likes of Muggsy McGraw. And it having to do with a woman! "Only one per cent of ballplayers are leaders of men," he declared once. "The other ninety-nine per cent are followers of women." And a bride! Here is the wives' tale he offered on that subject: "Very few ball players are ever as valuable to a team the first year they are married as they are before or after."

But then, he had begun to truly love the Mathewsons, as they were learning to love him. Growing up, McGraw had never had much of a family life — certainly not a happy one — and he had already had a childless marriage before he married Blanche. Probably he sensed by now that he must be sterile, that he could never sire a son of his own. His relationship with Mathewson was always so strange, and their ages were too close for McGraw to pose as a father figure, but Matty had already become, in some fashion, his boy, his kid brother — or maybe just his alter ego, the man Muggsy would have been if he had only been blessed, as a child, with books and looks and love.

EIGHT

No two boys could have had more different upbringings than Muggsy and Matty. Growing up, their only shared experience was as successful young ballplayers. Whereas Mathewson was raised comfortably in a sweet, settled home life, McGraw's dismal family experience of poverty and death seems more appropriate to Ireland itself, whence his father John left to escape poverty and death, than to the United States.

Not much is known of that older John McGraw's first years in America, except that he emigrated around 1856 and, during the Civil War, was drafted into the Union Army — a circumstance that many of his Irish brethren protested with riots. Why should they do the fighting in a war in which they had no real interest, where in fact they would be dying so that black men should be freed to compete with them for jobs? John McGraw also took a wife, probably shortly after being mustered out, probably in New York City, but she died giving birth to their first child, a daughter, and, so, with the baby girl, Anna, he headed upstate, settling in the village of Truxton, in Cortland County, then about an hour and a half's time south of Syracuse. It was there that he met and wed Ellen Comerford, who gave birth to their first child, a boy, who was John Joseph McGraw, born April 7, 1873.

The elder John McGraw was not an ignorant man. He had had many years of schooling in the Catholic schools of his native Ireland and sought work as a teacher. Although he was never close to his eldest son, we can imagine that he spoke highly about education to young Johnny; also, surely, he bewailed his fate that he himself could not find honest work at a school, but had to settle for laboring on the railroad. He was, it seems, a good man, who did his best by what became a brood of children. But also he was dull and dark and unimaginative. Certainly, like so many immigrant parents, he could not understand how his son could be so taken by a *game.*

Johnny McGraw, though, was absolutely captivated by baseball. He paid ten cents for a copy of *Our Boys Base Ball Rules* and became as much an authority about the game as he was a prodigy. He was a responsible kid, though, an altar boy who took odd jobs about town. Later he worked as a paperboy for the *Elmira Telegraph* and then as a butcher boy on his father's railroad, the Elmira, Cortland & Northern. There, days, he walked the aisles hawking snacks and magazines. Always, though — as we know from that episode where he earned his first professional dollar, pitching a curveball for the edification of train passengers — always Johnny carried his baseball with him. His first one cost a dollar, which he sent away to Spalding for. Other baseball expenses, earning even more of his father's ire, came when John Sr. had to pony up for windows broken on account of his son's slugging.

There was never enough money, always another mouth to nurse and feed. Ellen gave birth most years, the eighth arriving when Johnny was himself yet only eleven, in January of '85. Shortly after this last child was born, though, Ellen took deathly ill. It was very fast: diphtheria — or "black diphtheria" as it was often called then, when it was a scourge. Terribly infectious, highly contagious, a disease affecting the upper respiratory tract, diphtheria was all the more devastating in that it especially took down children. Ellen died in two days. Then Anna, the oldest, her stepchild. Three more of the McGraw babies fell after that.

Johnny was the oldest now in a motherless family. Three other small children and a newborn baby were left for the father to somehow tend to. In the world we like to imagine, the ghastly tragedy would have drawn the father and his eldest son together. It didn't. Ellen had been the connecting tissue. Now she was gone, the house was gripped in despair and malnourishment, and so, come the spring, Johnny's baseball became even more a bone of contention. Most everyone in Truxton would hear it: the incessant thudding of a Spalding pounding against the wall of a shed — Johnny McGraw, pitching, day after day. Later that year the boy broke another window, and his father could stand it no more. Erupting in a fury, he grabbed his son and, as the other children looked on in horror, it seemed as if he would beat him to death.

Somehow Johnny wrestled free from his father's grasp and departed the house, gone for good. He found refuge at the town's small hotel, where the proprietress took him in, giving him his keep in return for the chores she assigned him. He did remain in school, but like so many disadvantaged but athletic American teenagers who would follow his example ever since, he tended to his sport more than to his books. A dirt-poor, uneducated Irish kid living in the sticks — early on Muggsy must have seen his main chance.

How a boy with short arms who weighed barely a hundred pounds could pitch with any authority — how he could throw a curveball! — we don't know. But Johnny McGraw could. He taught himself that. In those days, almost every town in America had its own team and, it seems, residency was often winked at as a requirement of participation. Certainly it was by the summer of '89 when the hamlet of East Homer, nearby to Truxton, needed a pitcher. Johnny was approached. He drove a hard bargain: five bucks and round-trip transportation. So he was taken over from Truxton in a carriage, and he won the game, departing a hero from East Homer. After that, there was never any doubt what career path McGraw would follow, and the next spring, when he heard about a new minor league, the New York–Pennsylvania, he talked his way onto the team at Olean for forty dollars a month.

He was just turned seventeen years old when he left school, packed his valise, and took off on the journey down to Olean. He would find his way back to education, but never again did he return to stay in the only hometown he had ever known. Only he would never let himself forget the ghastly way he fought and lived as a child. He would not let those hard memories die. When he became successful, Muggsy always had a dog in his childless home, and every dog he owned — most of them Boston bull terriers — he would name "Truxton." And every morning, he would sit down with his dog and partake of the same breakfast: orange juice, scrambled eggs, bacon, toast, and coffee. He would feed his dog a little bit of bacon, and then this is the refrain John J. McGraw would scream out: "It's Truxton against the world!"

The Mathewsons were of Scottish descent — Mattesons, originally — arriving in Rhode Island way back in the seventeenth century. Matty's grandfather moved the family to Factoryville, Pennsylvania, in 1847, where he constructed a log cabin for his family. Factoryville, near Scranton, is also, by the by, almost directly due south of Truxton — not even two hours' time now down the present U.S. Interstate 81. The town was perhaps half-again Truxton's size, with six or seven hundred souls, when Christopher Mathewson came into this world at the family house on August 12, 1880. He was named for a childless uncle, who paid Matty's father a thousand dollars for the honor — the first instance, so far as we know, of naming rights being paid in baseball.

As for the name Factoryville, it is altogether misleading and was indeed detested by its rural residents. The place, you see, was hardly some smoky factory town. Instead, it was named for a cotton mill that failed early on. In point of fact, Factoryville was a bucolic place, green and altogether country, unsoiled by industry or by the mean anthracite fields that lay only a few miles south.

Mathewson's father, Gilbert, had, like McGraw's father, served in the Federal Army but, unlike the Irish immigrant, he had signed on willingly for the cause of union. Some years later he married Minerva Capwell — she from a family of means — and so they had a swell house in a valley as Mr. Mathewson practiced gentleman farming. A babbling brook flowed through the property. There was an apple orchard and farm animals, and little Christy learned to throw by chucking stones at blackbirds, sparrows, and squirrels. He would even attribute his fabulous control to what he learned, flinging at wildlife. As for his general athletic ability, that may have come primarily from his mother's side. Minerva was known as "Nervy" for having had the guts, as a kid, to break a giant of a mean, stubborn horse.

Christy was the first born. Another son, Cyril, came along two years later, but he died in infancy. This seems to be the only sadness that the happy Mathewson family had to endure while Christy was growing up, but it was quickly overcome by the arrival of other healthy children, all arriving precisely at two-year intervals: Christine in '84, Henry in '86, Jane in '88, and the baby Nicholas in '90. The Mathewsons were neat and organized. Christy picked up the trombone and played it in the town band. He was, of course, an excellent student and gave no trouble whatsoever at Keystone Academy, a local Baptist prep school founded by his own grandmother.

Christy's mother dreamed that her eldest son would find the calling and become a Baptist preacher. Here, Minerva

Mathewson explained, is how she raised him: "I was always particular about regular hours of sleep and plenty of plain, wholesome food, good milk, fresh air. And the Golden Rule."

Early on, though, "Husk," as he was called, was renowned in Factoryville for his pitching. As young as fourteen, strong but a bit knock-kneed, he was pulling in a dollar a game pitching, against much older opponents, for the Factoryville nine. The first time he was chosen to pitch for the town team was "the proudest day of my life," especially since he won his own game with a big hit. He batted cross-handed then, which came naturally, he decided, since he hoed the garden that way. Soon, although he was nowhere near as adept as McGraw at selling his talents, he was picking up another dollar pitching for Mill City, seven miles away. He was so good that on one occasion, when his mother said he couldn't pitch because he hadn't finished hoeing the family potato patch, his teammates came over, and, rather like Tom Sawyer's buddies whitewashing the fence, they finished working the field for him so that Matty could start against Honesdale.

Everything just seemed to flow so naturally for Christy Mathewson. When he was seventeen, walking around Scranton, the big city, staring at the sights, he dropped by a YMCA game. One of the teams was short a pitcher, and someone spotted Matty in the stands, eating peanuts. He was called down, "leaving quite three cents worth of peanuts" behind, put on the only uniform available, which was much too large for him, but (of course) he won the game, striking out fifteen. By the end of that summer he was making twenty dollars a month, plus his board, pitching semipro ball up at Honesdale. "This seemed like a princely sum," Mathewson said in recollection, "and I began to speak of J. P. Morgan and me." Soon he put his mind to it and stopped batting cross-handed. And then there was Bucknell and field goals and the class presidency and the Giants and Manager McGraw and Jane. No one ever worked any harder, but it all seemed so effortless, so obviously a matter of destiny.

The first professional game that John McGraw played in, at Olean, on May 18, 1890, he fielded the first ball hit to him at third and threw it away. He made seven more errors before the game mercifully concluded. He lasted five more games before Olean let him go, but somehow

McGraw found a smaller town and a lower classification — Wellsville in the Western New York League — and there, although playing infrequently, he managed to take the field at every position but catcher and, wielding what was called a "wagon tongue," he batted a handsome .365.

From Wellsville he caught on with a barnstorming team that played all over Cuba that winter in hideously bright yellow uniforms. A kid who had never been anyplace more exotic than Syracuse, McGraw found that he loved the travel, loved the adventure. He had never cared much for learning before, but now that he was out of Truxton, out on his own, he was drenched in curiosity. He adored Cuba, and thereafter he would regularly return. Indeed, McGraw is given credit for naming the joint in Havana so identified with Ernest Hemingway. As the story has it, McGraw would tease the owner, José Abeal, about his balloonlike sleeves, which would, McGraw groused, get in the way, "slopping up the place." Hence: Sloppy Joe's.

In 1912, on one of his many visits to Havana, he discovered daiquiris at the famous La Floridita Bar, and so familiar a patron was he that the proprietor named another rum drink after him, calling it the "Jota Jota" — using the two Js in McGraw's initials. Apparently it remained on the bar menu at La Floridita for more than another half century, until Fidel Castro, that knowledgeable baseball aficionado, found out what the Js stood for and demanded that any such drink named for a Yanqui ballplayer be expunged.

In 1890, though, the seventeen-year-old McGraw didn't drink. Maybe he had lost his virginity in a Havana whorehouse. He sure as hell hadn't in Olean or Wellsville. He never did smoke. "You'll find cigarette stubs on the guideposts to baseball oblivion," he once declared. Never in his life could he even tolerate a woman who smoked. But back then, all he wanted was the chance to play ball, and luckily for him, when the pickup team he was with came back to the States, it played an exhibition game in Florida against the big league club from Cleveland and McGraw got three hits. Reports of the cheeky little scuffler got out, and he went to Iowa for seventy-five dollars a month to play for the Cedar Rapids Canaries. He hit a respectable, if not spectacular, .285 there, attracting the attention of a Baltimore scout who was looking for players for manager Bill Barnie.

"You can tell Barnie I'm just about as good as they come," McGraw declared, and sure enough he was invited to move up to the Orioles. Muggsy had managed to go from signing a contract in Truxton when he was still sixteen years old to making the big leagues in only sixteen months, when he was yet just eighteen.

As quickly as he took to Baltimore and thought of it as home, though, McGraw soon began spending much of his off-season back in New York state. During his brief, dispiriting sojourn at Olean, he had met a young Franciscan priest, Father Joseph F. Dolan, who was on the faculty at nearby Allegany College (which would become St. Bonaventure). Following the 1892 season, McGraw began a correspondence with Father Dolan, and eventually they struck a deal: if McGraw would help coach the college's baseball team during the winter (using the basement of one of the little school's three buildings), he would be provided room and board and be allowed to take courses for free.

He signed up for English grammar and composition, history, and mathematics, and became a devoted student who eventually made the honor roll. Indeed, so well did the arrangement work that not only did McGraw return to college the next winter, but he brought Hughie Jennings along with him. This was the winter when McGraw taught Jennings not to shy away from inside pitches. It was the start of something even more profound for Jennings, too, for while he was no more schooled than McGraw — having grown up in a poor mining family in Pittston, Pennsylvania, not far from Mathewson's hometown — Jennings continued with his education to the point where he eventually gained a law degree.

This made McGraw tremendously proud — perhaps especially because he never earned enough credits for his own degree. Nonetheless, although it is impossible to know how much the four winters spent at college taught him, they clearly gave him a grounding in the culture and a confidence in society that he otherwise would never have enjoyed. He became more secure, able to comfortably counter the stereotype of the time of the dumb and drunken Mick . . . and/or the dumb and drunken ballplayer. Perhaps just as important, McGraw never showed the resentment to college-boy players that others of his background did. It seems almost impossible that he could have ever become close to Mathewson had he not himself also spent some time, seriously, at higher education. Just as Blanche McGraw felt so sure that Jane Mathewson — who had attended a coordinate female institution with Bucknell — must be looking down her nose at her, so surely did McGraw sometimes feel diminished in certain company. But he had been to college, he had studied the likes of Latin, literature, geometry, and history — and in his speech and his references, he came across as the educated man. And he truly was, even if he also remained coarse and bellicose all his life (although, most generously, Matty said only that McGraw's "oratory would make a Billingsgate fishwife sore").

Nothing infuriated Muggsy more than when others put down ballplayers as truant dopes. It is instructive that, when he wrote his memoirs, out of the blue, the *very* first subject he chose to discuss was education. He began his book by explaining that he has always sought college boys because such a type "tries to find his faults" while "the unschooled fellow usually tries to hide his."

Invariably, whenever McGraw was asked to assess the demands of baseball, he paid as much attention to the requirements of the mind as of the body. The Reverend Christian Reisier of Grace Methodist Episcopal Church on West 104th Street always gave an annual baseball sermon, which would be attended by some of the Protestant Giants or Yankees. In 1913, before the Giants played the A's in the World Series, the Reverend Mr. Reisier took to the pulpit the subject of "Who Will Win?" Specifically, he cited Mathewson as "the finest illustration of the well-pressured man," adding the innocent canard that young Matty had been introduced to the game by a Methodist minister.

Naturally, the papist McGraw could not be expected to worship in such a heathen venue, but he did accept the minister's invitation to write to the parishioners about the value of the great game. Here was his summary of the sport he loved: "Naturally, I think baseball is the most admirable pastime in the world . . . a keen combination of wit, intelligence and muscle. . . . It develops the mind, establishes discipline and gives to those who take part in it sound bodies, clear heads and a better sense of life." To Muggsy, baseball was never just sport. It was important to him that he credited it as an uplifting experience.

His own college education concluded

after the winter of '95, though, because after Baltimore won the pennant again in '96, he rounded up some of his Oriole buddies and off they went on a grand tour of Europe. Along with Keeler, Jennings, and Kelley, McGraw also invited the team's most erudite member, Arlie Pond, a young pitcher who was studying medicine at Johns Hopkins (indeed, he would soon enough desert baseball to become an army surgeon, serving for many years in the Philippines). The five Orioles steamed to Liverpool, where, to his dismay, McGraw overslept on the Sunday after their arrival so that he missed mass for the first time in many Sundays. But, notwithstanding this spiritual lapse, he led the troupe on, to London, Amsterdam, Brussels, and Paris.

McGraw was as taken by Europe as he had been by Cuba. There would be more trips abroad for such a genuine world traveler. Muggsy was becoming something of a dandy, too, favoring a fancy stickpin in his tie, carrying a gold-headed cane, and wearing a medallion on his watch chain that Cardinal Gibbons himself had given him. Now, too, Muggsy added a Continental touch, arriving back in Baltimore decked out in gentleman's style from head to toe, in a silk top hat, custom-made boots, and a Prince Albert coat.

Muggsy McGraw was not just a collegian. He had become a man of the world. Eventually, in fact, it was he who would encourage the educated Mr. Mathewson to widen his own horizons and join him abroad, too.

NINE

The infirmities that would dog McGraw for the rest of his life first struck him in the '95 season, when he was only twenty-two years old. The diagnosis was malaria, and although he was forced to miss thirty-five games, he still hit .369 and the Orioles repeated as champions.

The next season was almost a complete loss, though. Indeed, he almost died of typhoid fever, which he contracted in spring training. He grew violently ill when the team stopped in Atlanta, but luckily, Arlie Pond, the medical student, realized the severity of McGraw's case and took him to a hospital. The team moved on north while McGraw remained in the hospital in Atlanta with a high fever that would not abate. It was June before he was allowed to leave the hospital, but by then his weight had dropped from a robust 155 down to 118. He still could not walk without crutches and was forced to continue his recuperation down the Chesapeake, at a resort hotel in Old Point Comfort, Virginia.

It was August before McGraw rejoined the team. While he was as cantankerous as ever — "His appearance put new life into the team," the *Baltimore Morning Herald* noted, adding: "There is only one McGraw, and he is a revelation" — his near-fatal disease brought him up short. As Burt Solomon, the Old Oriole historian, wrote: "There was nothing like a brush with death to show a man that some things are more precious than a game." It was that fall when Muggsy led his teammates across the Atlantic, and upon his return he and Uncle Robbie got the Diamond Café up and running. More important, at some time in the latter part of '96, he began romancing Minnie Doyle, the twenty-year-old brunette daughter of a retired court clerk. Minnie may well have introduced herself to McGraw by sending him a letter with compressed flowers when he was convalescing.

In the event, he started calling on her sometime after he came back to Baltimore, and then, with his European travels behind him and his new business venture under way, Muggsy proposed to Minnie. They were married in downtown Baltimore on a frigid winter's day, February 3, 1897. McGraw chose Jennings as his best man, with the other Oriole stalwarts in attendance. Indeed, despite the freezing weather, it was SRO in the church, a real celebrity wedding. However, not a single member of McGraw's own family was at the ceremony. Nonetheless, when the happy couple went off to Niagara Falls on their honeymoon, they swung by Truxton, where Muggsy introduced his bride to his father. It was rare that he ever saw his old man, but at least the pain of the past was forgotten. McGraw was a man who famously carried grudges; notwithstanding, if he was never close to his father, neither did he hold him in enmity once he had left home and found his fortune.

He and Minnie returned to Baltimore, there to start a family, as the Orioles sought a fourth straight championship. Neither would come to pass. At least McGraw did not suffer any illness in '97, but he did endure two serious injuries, and however happy he was as a bridegroom, he was more nettlesome than ever around the diamond. Once, he and Keeler got into a clubhouse brawl when both men were as naked as jaybirds (and Wee Willie, apparently, got the best of Muggsy). He gave no quarter to umpires whatsoever.

John Heydler would later become president of the National League but at this time was on the league's umpiring staff. It is hard to imagine how much umpires despised McGraw, but this is Heydler's woeful recollection: "The Orioles were mean, vicious, ready at any time to maim a rival player or an umpire if it helped their cause. The things they said to umpires were unbelievably vile, and they broke the spirits of some fine men. I've seen umpires bathe their feet by the hour after McGraw and others spiked them. . . . The lot of the umpires never was worse than in the years the Orioles were flying high."

McGraw was the obvious choice to replace Hanlon in '99 as the Orioles manager, and he did an amazing job of keeping the depleted team in the pennant race. If he got too tough on the boys, Uncle Robbie would smooth things out. "Robbie was the sugar and I was the vinegar," was how Muggsy explained it. He was always up to some new trick. Once, when he was coaching third in a close game against Brooklyn, he called over to the Superbas pitcher and asked to see the ball. Without thinking, the pitcher tossed the ball to McGraw, who simply stepped aside in the coacher's box and let the ball roll away as the Oriole base runner dashed into scoring position.

Perhaps the only off-putting part of the summer was Minnie's stomach pains. They came and went, and nobody seemed to know what to make of them. Then, on August 26, when the Orioles were in Louisville, Minnie's pain became so unbearable that doctors had to come to the house. They diagnosed appendicitis so acute that they dared not move her to a hospital, but surgeons from Johns Hopkins came to the house on St. Paul Street in order to remove the appendix there.

McGraw got the telegram in the midst of a doubleheader and took the first train back from Louisville. By the time he reached Baltimore, the operation had gone smoothly and it appeared to be a success. Muggsy rushed to see her, there in the bed they shared. Alas, three nights later Minnie began to suffer with blood poisoning. McGraw sat with his wife by their bed all that night and into the next morning until finally Minnie Doyle McGraw slipped peacefully into death. She was twenty-two years old and was buried in her wedding gown.

The young widower McGraw did not

come back to the team for another two weeks, and it was ten days after that before he put himself in a game. For the first time, people noticed that he had gray hairs. He wasn't yet thirty years old. He had lost his mother and four of his sisters and brothers, and now, after almost having died himself, he had lost his wife. All from disease.

It is not so surprising, then, that some years later, when Mathewson fell seriously ill, McGraw grew quickly disturbed, behaving even more erratically. This was near the end of spring training in 1906. Mathewson fell sick in Memphis with what at first appeared to be only a bad cold. Soon, however, his illness was diagnosed as diphtheria, although this alarming information seems to have been kept from the public; only oblique references to "his illness" were made in the press. His travail was closely followed, though. MATTY WALKS! headlined the *Evening World* on that occasion when at last he became ambulatory.

When Mathewson finally returned to the pitcher's box on May 5, attracting a huge midweek crowd of fifteen thousand on a miserably wet afternoon, the *Times* still attributed his absence of more than a month only to "a rather severe cold." The throng, said the *Tribune*, "rose en masse to give him a standing ovation," and Mathewson responded with a fairly good effort against the Beaneaters, or, as the *Herald* would have them, "the savants from the grove of Academe." Matty gave up three runs and seven hits in seven innings, and left with a lead, but McGinnity blew it in relief. Nevertheless, said the *World*, "the great pitcher proved that he retained his grip on the hearts of New Yorkers."

All along, though, McGraw was aware of the true nature of Matty's malady; he knew it was diphtheria from the moment it was diagnosed. Muggsy was beside himself. For much of that time, Matty had been quarantined. It was especially important to keep him away from Jane, who was pregnant. Telephones were in general use now, and McGraw stayed in constant touch with Matty and Jane and the doctors. It did not seem possible that it could happen to him again, that someone else he loved would be taken from him. His behavior grew more erratic than ever. His "constant bickering only brings discredit," the *Tribune* chastised him. He was "overindulgent in conversation" with the umpires, regularly "calling [them] names from the bench" and making "useless objections." They were not just incompetent; now they were *thieves*.

Thieves! Harry Pulliam, the young National League president, grew angrier and more frustrated at each more egregious McGravian transgression. Muggsy was thrown out of more games, even drawing a three-game suspension. In Providence, for a mere exhibition game, about the time Mathewson was conclusively diagnosed with diphtheria, McGraw went completely haywire, taking the whole team off the field in protest over some ordinary decision. The furious spectators started to descend on the Giants, who were obliged to brandish their bats in defense. Finally the umpires prevailed on McGraw to finish the exhibition.

Muggsy had become a drinker by now. This time, when Matty was sick and maybe dying, was a time when too often he started drinking too much.

TEN

The 1890s, when John J. McGraw came to national prominence, were known not only as the Gay Nineties, but also the Electric Nineties, the Romantic Nineties, possibly even the Moulting Nineties. Together with the beginning of the twentieth century, the period was known as the Banquet Years, or the Mauve Decades (don't ask). The era began with the terrible economic Panic of '93, and the nation was bifurcated then as now by region, as underscored by William Jennings Bryan and his cross-of-gold theatrics. But once beyond the economic travails, as the century turned, Lord, did the country start busting its buttons.

The United States was, if gingerly, taking on the trappings of empire, managing that with the chips it took off the table from Spain. Then there was gold in Alaska, and soon enough a bull in the china shop in the White House. Perhaps nothing illustrated the rambunctious nature of the times more than the big hit of '98, the favorite of all the Spanish-American War bands: "They'll Be a Hot Time in the Old Town To-Night." It was a nation of obstreperous strivers. "America, as yet, had no place for the idle rich, chiefly because there had been, as yet, no idle rich," observed Mark Sullivan. The humorist Finley Peter Dunne, writing in an Irish accent as the famous Mr. Dooley, declared that "the crownin' wurruk iv our civilization — th' cash raygister."

Still, America remained agrarian. As the new century began, 60 percent of Americans resided on farms or in small towns. Good grief, there were still two thousand individual farms in New York City, and as late as 1908 wild goats roamed Fifth Avenue, around 90th Street, just north of the magnificent mansions that lined the country's most famous boulevard.

But more and more Americans were moving to the cities — not only coming from the countryside, like McGraw and Mathewson, but also from abroad — turning them into (as the brand-new term suggested) "melting pots." A new type of city dweller began to emerge. Among other things, since the six-day, sixty-hour-a-week work was growing shorter, there was more time for leisure — specifically for our purposes: more opportunity to attend baseball games. The boom in stadium attendance in the first decade of the new century probably had as much to do with more leisure opportunity as it did with any better brand of baseball.

Henry Adams described this fresh new urban American thusly: "[He was] a pushing, energetic, ingenious person, always awake and trying to get ahead of his neighbors . . . work and whiskey were his stimulants; work was a form of vice; he never cared much for money or power after he earned them. The amusement of the pursuit was all the amusement he got from it."

All of that — well, except for the business about not caring for the power — fit John J. McGraw to a tee. It is ironic that whereas Matty would become the first great American sports hero, Muggsy was much more representative of the rampant young American male of the Mauve Decades. Matty was the all-American boy grown up; Muggsy was the all-American striver (or, well, hustler). It wasn't just that he made a life out of baseball, out of a game; he made sure to make a lot of money out of it, too. "From the start,"

Blanche Sindall McGraw wrote, "I saw him as a young man of indestructible confidence, ever of visible optimism and hope, but not of the Pollyanna variety."

She first met him a year after Minnie died, when he and Hughie Jennings — himself also already a widower — were invited by a friend to come by the Sindalls' fine house for a party. McGraw and Jennings were both out of mourning, Muggsy back from that one rare relaxing season in St. Louis, where he made a lot of money without expending much energy. Blanche's first impression was that the famous young man was "courteous and self-assured." Well, away from the diamond, he usually did strike folks as a different breed of cat.

Blanche was only nineteen, almost a decade his junior. She had sable eyes and hair to match, was barely five feet tall, and what we knew then as "pleasingly plump." It was the fashion; Lillian Russell, the grandest female star in show business, weighed in at a hefty 165. She just ate like a horse and tightened her corset. Blanche, like Jane Mathewson, was also a rare college girl for that time, attending St. Agnes College for Young Women.

But then, Blanche's father, James, was a

prosperous businessman. Minnie Doyle's father had been only a dour government functionary, a widower, up in years. James Sindall was a vigorous self-made man who had started out selling stoves and then took out on his own as a contractor. The Sindalls lived in a house James Sindall had built himself; it was, as Baltimoreans are wont to say, "out" York Road, in the fashionable new Waverly area. McGraw was not only admiring of James Sindall, but even a little intimidated by him; the toughest ballplayer in the land took several months getting up the nerve to ask for Sindall's daughter's hand in marriage. But McGraw not only fell in love with Blanche, he adored the whole Sindall family. He'd never really been part of a big, happy family before, and had, as Blanche put it, "a gnawing hunger" for such a thing.

Indeed, for all that was going on in McGraw's life as 1900 passed into '01 — as he became the linchpin for the new Baltimore franchise in the new American League — he courted Blanche leisurely. He brought her flowers regularly. They both loved to go to vaudeville and musicals downtown, and worshiped at St. Ann's together. The Sindalls were not Irish; they were of Dutch heritage, but they were staunch Roman Catholics. Blanche knew nothing of baseball when the romance began, but things were certainly progressing nicely by the spring. For Opening Day, the Orioles' first game in the new American League, with Ban Johnson throwing out the first ball himself, from all of Baltimore to pick from, it was the Sindall family that manager John McGraw chose to invite to sit in his box.

Now that the season had begun, McGraw's favorite escape from his baseball duties was to take out the Sindall family carriage, meandering through Druid Hill Park with Blanche by his side. It could not have been more innocent; they would stop for ice cream sodas. Curiously, McGraw always had Blanche hold the reins on the mare, Fanny. For whatever reason, in all his life, horses or cars, McGraw never liked to drive. It was just one of those things; he certainly wanted to run everything else. Mathewson on the other hand fancied cars as soon as they came into fashion and, to Jane's dismay, was even something of a daredevil behind the wheel. In 1912 he would be fined a hundred dollars for whipping along at thirty-one miles per hour in a car given him by his adoring fans. At the ballpark, it was Matty's signature to walk from the clubhouse to the diamond wearing an automobile driver's long white linen duster over his uniform.

McGraw, though, was at heart really something of an old-fashioned fellow. He never even took to moving pictures. For that matter, as he grew older, he wouldn't be very good at adapting to the new manner of ballplayers. As cagey as McGraw was, he was pretty set in his ways by the time he fell in love with Blanche. The way the world turned when the Orioles were riding high was the way he liked it. We don't think that hard-boiled types can be sentimentalists, but McGraw put the lie to that stereotype. The meaner McGraw got, the sweeter the past seemed to him. And, if he didn't realize it then, the past essentially ended on January 8, 1902, when he married Blanche at St. Ann's.

It had been only five years, shy a month, since he had married Minnie, and many of the same players returned, principals in this wedding party, too (Wee Willie gave the couple silver oyster forks). Keeler and those other Old Oriole teammates standing up for McGraw could barely stifle their laughter, too, as the presiding priest, Father Cornelius Thomas, felt obliged to wrench baseball into his charge to the newlyweds.

"Let selfishness be no barrier to your happiness, but understand that each must give up much, renounce himself, that both may enjoy delightful fruit," he began conventionally enough. But then: "For you know that it is the sacrifice hit that adds to the number of runs and wins in the game."

And to McGraw (as his groomsmen snickered): "Lead her around the hard 'bases' of life until she reaches the 'home plate' of happiness. . . . The church 'signs' her over to you. You will not have trouble to 'manage' her."

And Muggsy didn't. He ran the marriage as he did his ball club, calling all the pitches. Blanche was his most ardent defender; she trusted him implicitly. Even though he was promiscuous with loans and given to making atrocious investments, Mrs. McGraw did not complain. "I never knew the exact nature of John McGraw's financial philosophy, and I never worried about it," she blithely explained. "He gave me everything I ever asked for or failed to ask for. I wanted for nothing, and so I never questioned his income or what he did with it."

It was only a few months into their marriage when the Oriole franchise began to founder, when Muggsy began to look for a way out of Baltimore, secretly taking trains up to New York to meet with Andrew Freedman. If McGraw let on that he might be taking Blanche away from the city where she had resided all her life, he didn't tell her much. "My job was faith," is how Blanche described the situation. Then, when McGraw did take her in tow to New York, she looked upon it as a grand adventure. Like her new husband, Blanche adapted quickly to the bustle and delights of the big town.

Much would be made of the fact that Babe Ruth and the Yankees were so perfect a match for the New York of the Roaring Twenties, but it's just as accurate to say that it was only appropriate that Muggsy and Matty gave Gotham baseball glory when they did. Turn-of-the-century New York was exploding. It had, it seemed, everything else but a winning baseball club, and once Brooklyn and the other boroughs were consolidated with Manhattan, the city's population soared to almost three and a half million. Only London in all the world was larger, but more tellingly: New York used four times the electricity that London did. The gaslights were going out all over.

Ground-breaking for the city's first subway line, which would run from city hall, near the bottom of Manhattan Island, all the way up to 145th Street — felicitously for the Giants, not that far from the Polo Grounds — took place in March 1900. "Fifteen minutes to Harlem!" was the somewhat optimistic boast; but hey, it really would take only twenty-six. It was a wondrous advance for New Yorkers. Looking back, one historian would write: "Only Armistice Day, V-E Day, V-J Day and the return of Charles Lindbergh . . . produced as enthusiastic an explosion of public joy." But then, even before the subway had opened for business on October 27, 1904, the aboveground railroads in New York were already carrying more passengers than all the other steam trains in both North and South America. Cars were rapidly replacing horses. In 1895 there were perhaps 300 automobiles in New York; a decade later there were 78,000. If you had to get outta town, the 20th Century Limited averaged forty-nine miles per hour and could deposit you in Chicago in twenty hours. If you were a letter, you could get to San Francisco in four days. Long-distance could put you through to Omaha. President Roosevelt sent a telegraph message clear 'round the world in 1903.

New York had the largest hotel in the world — the Waldorf-Astoria — 1,100 rooms, 765 baths. It had the tallest building — an amazing twenty-nine stories high, soaring above Park Row. The Metropolitan Opera had opened in 1887, Carnegie Hall in '91, and the Bronx Zoo in '99. Construction on the New York Public Library would begin in 1902, about the time the McGraws got off the train from Baltimore and checked into the Victoria Hotel. Macy's also opened in '02, bringing the best shopping area farther uptown from the "Ladies' Mile," which had topped out at Twenty-third Street. New theaters were springing up, too, and Longacre Square became Times Square in 1904 (the first New Year's ball dropped in 1908). Also, there were twenty-five thousand prostitutes ("It costs a dollar, and I've got a room").

The poor and disenfranchised poured in from abroad, making New York a city more variegated in its human splendor than any ever on earth. In the first decade of the twentieth century, almost a million immigrants a year came in. On April 11,

1903, just a few days before the Giants began their first full season under McGraw, a record ten thousand newcomers arrived at Ellis Island on that one day. Many would remain in New York, which was now 37 percent foreign-born (and another 38 percent of the residents had at least one foreign-born parent). Jacob Riis, the reformer, noted: "A map of the city, colored to designate minorities, would show more stripes than on the skin of a zebra and more colors than any rainbow."

Something like 800,000 Germans were in the city, most clustered in downtown Manhattan in what was called Kleindeutschland. There were 275,000 Irish, 220,000 Italians, 60,000 blacks, and perhaps 700,000 Jews from all nations. The German Jews, looking down their noses at their spiritual cousins from eastern Europe, had started calling them "kikes," from the many names that ended in *ki*. But then, most stage comedy was ethnic; so too the humorous newspaper columns. Everybody got by, laughing at everybody else. Everybody else's sister in every other minority was a slut. Everybody but the Jews drank too much. And every mother's son took up baseball, tossing whatever would pass for a ball over and around the two thousand pushcarts that filled the slum streets, peddling clothing, household goods, and (mostly spoiled) produce. When the price of a standard block of ice was doubled to sixty cents, it created a huge furor, far greater than any fuss made nowadays about higher gasoline prices. The summer heat was unbearable; going up to the Polo Grounds was like escaping to Maine. Even then, the players' heavy flannel uniforms might gain as much as eight or ten pounds of sweat during a game.

Manhattan was straining at its limits. That plot of land on a hill way uptown — where Columbia Presbyterian Hospital is now located — was virtually the only place on the whole island that the owners of the new American League franchise could find in 1903 to build their ballyard. Downtown, a million and a half people were crowded together on the Lower East Side, 500,000 of those in one square mile, the densest human habitation in the world. It was estimated that two-thirds of Manhattan residents were jammed into six-story tenements — mostly known as "dumbbells" — which held 150 people apiece. The local anthem, "The Sidewalks of New

York," written in '94 by a blind buck-and-wing dancer named Charles Lawler, tried to make romantic of what was nearly intolerable: "East side, west side, all around the town . . . we would sing and waltz, / While the 'ginnie' played the organ on the sidewalks of New York."

When Blanche and Muggsy first arrived, he would go to work at the Polo Grounds (on the days he didn't go to the racetrack first) by taking a horse-drawn hack, moseying up through Central Park and into Harlem. At that time the area was mostly middle-class Irish and German with some Jews, but speculation in new housing exceeded demand when the city's first subway line was built up that way, so the building owners were forced to sell to anybody they could. That was how the African-American migration to Harlem began.

Ah, and Muggsy's own folk. The Irish were starting to move up the scale. For so long they had performed much of the dirty, unskilled work, building up New York — tunneling that first subway, for example. The joke was that an Irishman turned down a higher-paying job as a diver because he couldn't spit on his hands before he began that work. But with the new immigrants coming from southern and eastern Europe, the Irish finally had someone below them in the pecking order. They became the foremen, bossing Italians about. Onstage, many of the Pat-and-Mike jokes became Abie-and-Sol jokes. As early as 1890, a third of the city's teachers were Irish women, and that stereotypical Irish cop was, it seems, walking every beat, chomping on free apples. *"Good marnin' to ya, officer." "Ah, and the same ta you, Mrs. O'Flaherty."*

Not only that but, of course, the Irish began to accumulate power, moving up from street gangs, taking a conspicuous place in Tammany Hall. For national prominence, though, the first Irish mark was in sports. The heavyweight title seemed to absolutely belong to a Son of Erin: Paddy Ryan, the Great John L., Gentleman Jim Corbett, Bob Fitzgibbons, James J. Jeffries. But if Gentleman Jim, anyway, was a social cut above (it was he who introduced the highfalutin term "solar plexus" into boxing), the so-called sweet science, then as now, was more of a déclassé divertissement, and for all that baseballists were supposed to be drunkards, whoremongers, and unreliable reprobates, the game — *the game!* — was becoming nearly sacred, the American national sport. "Because baseball was the country's most popular sport, closely linked to the image of a rural Protestant nation," wrote one New York Irish historian, "Irish players came to represent American adaptability, and their skills in this arena gave them a more acceptable persona than boxing prowess." In other words, for all that the Irish put into baseball, they took more out.

As early as 1890, when one Bill McGunnigle managed the Brooklyn Bridegrooms, the Irish had a leadership beachhead in New York baseball. Foxy Ned Hanlon would, of course, guide Brooklyn (now the Superbas) to the National League pennants of '99 and '00. But when McGraw grasped the Giant reins in '02, quickly establishing front-office hegemony to go with his field command, Irish pride reached new heights. Soon enough, with the possible exception of his good pal George M. Cohan, John J. McGraw would become the most famous Irish-American in the land. His Giants teams were not nearly so Irish as had been his Orioles. McGraw would hire any scoundrel he thought could help him win; he was forever bringing back Turkey Mike Donlin. But the Irish imprint on the Giants was strong.

McGraw was no crusader, either, but in 1901, when the color line in baseball was well established, Muggsy tried to sign an American Indian player, Chief Tokohama, for the Orioles. Only Chief Tokohama was no Indian. The White Stockings owner, Charles Comiskey, a dreadful human being whose parsimony would lead to his players fixing the 1919 World Series, blew the whistle on the Chief, revealing him to be an African-American bellhop whom McGraw had "fixed up with war paint and a bunch of feathers." In 1923, when Babe Ruth, the Sultan of Swat, was drawing attention to the Yankees, away from the Giants, McGraw found a fellow named Mose Solomon playing Class C ball in Kansas and introduced him to the Polo Grounds faithful as the "Rabbi of Swat." Alas, the Rabbi lasted only two desultory games, failing to attract throngs of New York Hebrews.

And, of course, McGraw's greatest player and largest gate attraction was the Presbyterian farm boy, Mathewson. Neither would have become so famous without the other. No coach can succeed, no matter how intrinsically good, without a winning team. Mathewson could have won for anybody, but that he had McGraw's Giants behind him, playing in New York, gave him all the more fame than he ever would have gained, say, had he honored that contract with Connie Mack's Athletics down in Philadelphia. Rather, both men found the moment — Mathewson arriving as professional baseball became more respectable, and McGraw taking charge as, likewise, the Irish were gaining a foot-hold in society.

Irish esteem increased all the more when the phonograph player began to move into homes and, starting in 1906, Americans began to listen to the great tenor, John McCormack, singing indigenous Irish ballads that had never before been heard in the general population — the likes of "The Lily of Killarney," "The Wearing of the Green," and "Kathleen Mavourneen." McGraw was, not surprisingly, a sucker for Irish songs. Sunday nights, the McGraws enjoyed sing-alongs at home, with the host himself favoring "Break the News to Mother" and "Silver Threads among the Gold." But as often as he would go out to dinner dances, to fine restaurants that featured dancing with dinner, Blanche could never get him up on the floor except for one song. Muggsy would dance with his lady only when the band played "When Irish Eyes Are Smiling."

ELEVEN

The cracker barrel, where those legendary cracker-barrel philosophers held court, was for all intents and purposes made instantly obsolescent in 1898. That was when Uneeda brought out a package of crackers that cost five cents. If you could buy your own crackers in a handy package, who needed a barrel to dig into?

Uneeda knew pricing. The nickel was king in America at this time. It was so common a currency that the dime was, often as not, called a "double nickel." You didn't want to get stuck with a wooden nickel. The ultimate depth of worthlessness was a plugged nickel. What this country needed was a good five-cent cigar. At a time when laborers in New York made twenty cents an hour and a good meal would set you back fifteen cents, you could go into a saloon and, for a nickel, get a stein of beer and free bread, salami, pickled herring, and hard-boiled eggs for the asking. *"Barkeep, I'll have another beer."* When the subway opened up, naturally a ride was pegged at a nickel. This was the same as for streetcars, which particularly crisscrossed Brooklyn, so the players had to be nimble to negotiate streets to reach the ballpark: hence, the borough's team of Trolley Dodgers. The new movies not only charged a nickel, but were not called what they were, but what they cost: nickelodeons. A cuppa coffee cost a nickel. So did a soft drink. *"A Moxie, please."* *"Sure thing, mister, that'll be a nickel."* Ice cream was a nickel. Likewise a Tootsie Roll.

Did Jack Norworth — who, as we know, had never seen a baseball game when he wrote "Take Me Out to the Ball Game" — know that Cracker Jack cost a nickel when he threw it into his masterpiece just because he needed something to rhyme with *back?* (Otherwise, surely he would have written: "Buy me some peanuts and popcorn" — right?) Well, Cracker Jack, which had been introduced at the World's Columbian Exposition in Chicago in 1893 by two German immigrant brothers, one of whom cried out "That's a crackerjack of an idea!" — indeed sold for a nickel (although sans any prize — they weren't included until 1912).

However, if you too have been taken out to the ball game recently, you know of course that once you get in, you're a captive consumer, so everything costs more than on the outside. So it was then, too, at the Polo Grounds, that the vendors in black coats and white aprons charged double nickels for most of their wares — hot dogs, pieces of pie, beer, and, presumably, Cracker Jack. (Well, scorecards held the line at five cents.) Admission, too, did not come cheap. Box seats went for a buck twenty-five. General admission was half a dollar, and the cheapest bleacher seats were pegged at two bits. A large part of that distant territory was known as "Berkeville," since so many Irish sat out there.

These heady prices would account for why so many spectators would seek the limited vantage afforded by Coogan's Bluff, which overlooked the stadium. The Polo Grounds itself, lying under Coogan's Bluff, was originally Coogan's Hollow, the farm and salt fields of James J. Coogan, who was the first borough president of Manhattan (and a failed mayoral candidate).

Question: When did they play polo at the Polo Grounds?

Answer: They never did.

Question: Really? Then why —

Answer: It's sort of like nowadays when so many people wear polo shirts, even though they have never played polo (including Ralph Lauren).

But, you see, there was an earlier real Polo Grounds, located around 110th Street, by the northern extremities of Central Park, where polo was indeed contested. This property was owned by James Gordon Bennett, the newspaper publisher. The original New York Metropolitans adapted the polo fields there as their diamond home from 1883 to 1885, and so too the Giants, who had been the Troy Haymakers when they moved to Manhattan in 1883. When the Giants then moved up to Coogan's Hollow in 1889, they more or less brought the Polo Grounds name along with them. (The same sort of thing happened with Madison Square Garden, which has kept its original connection to Madison Avenue long after it started moving about town.)

The wooden Polo Grounds had a capacity of about sixteen thousand, but from the very beginning, tucked there under Coogan's Bluff, it had a bizarre configuration — short down the foul lines, then slanting sharply out to a center field that reached up to five hundred feet away, where, beyond, the Giants had their home dressing quarters. It was in those far environs where Willie Mays would make his fabled catch of Vic Wertz's long fly ball in the '54 Series, just as the stadium's short foul lines were immortalized by Bobby Thomson's pop-fly home run to left to win the '51 pennant against the Dodgers. (These sorts of hits were called "Chinese home runs" — meaning cheap — in those less sensitive times.)

None of this geography much mattered back then, though, when there were so few home runs hit and just about everybody played what might be called Muggsy Ball. (Hilltop Park, where the Yankees first played, had even more antic dimensions of 365-542-400.) Besides, spacious center fields provided a place for the well-heeled cranks to park their carriages. In all ballyards in those days, overflow crowds were allowed into the outfield, roped off. Hits popped into this human efflux were marked as ground-rule doubles or triples; better to sell more tickets than to keep the game pristine. Why, the Giants could accommodate as many as another four or five thousand standees in the outfield.

Until the subway was opened in 1904, the cheapest, fastest way to get to the game was on the Sixth Avenue elevated line. The trains could only go up to twenty miles an hour, however, because any greater speed would cause the track's superstructure to shimmy something awful. Still, it was pretty convenient. When the subway came in, it did forty-five miles an hour, and a "baseball special" from Wall Street made only one intermediate stop, at Forty-second Street. If you didn't have to work that day, you could drift up the Harlem River by excursion boat. Or, if you were flush, you and some buddies could rent a horse-drawn coach. That cost a dollar for the first mile, forty cents each additional, and forty cents for each fifteen-minute waiting period. It's cheaper than it sounds, too, because there wasn't a lot of lollygagging in those days once the deep-throated man with the megaphone announced the lineups, so most games were comfortably completed in less than two hours. Since the games started at three-thirty or four, any crank cum fan could be home to his mutton dinner or standing with a foot on the bar rail at a very reasonable hour indeed.

(In fact, nobody ever knew, back then,

how good they had it. When baseball juiced up the balls some in 1911, putting cork in the center, this helped the batters enough so that there were more hits, and a love-struck Ring Lardner, covering the games for a Chicago paper, wrote his fiancée: "It appears to be impossible to finish a game in less than two hours. It's bad enough now, but it's going to drive me crazy when it keeps me away from my home." Could Lardner ever have imagined that his press box descendants would be held captive for *three* hours, even *more?*)

Living together their first full season with the Giants, 1903, McGraw and Mathewson would, midday, bid Blanche and Jane good-bye and hie to the park. Notwithstanding Muggsy getting clobbered by the ball Dummy Taylor threw, it was a glorious time for them both. Mathewson won thirty games for the first time, age twenty-three. McGraw was just thirty, but he only embellished his managerial reputation, taking the Giants from the '02 cellar, with forty-eight wins, to second place behind the redoubtable Pittsburgh nine, with eighty-four victories. Overnight the city's attitude about the Giants changed.

Despite the fact that the Giants couldn't

catch the Pirates, McGraw (and John Brush, the new owner) began to envision a lucrative postseason exhibition series against Pittsburgh — Senior Circuit number one vs. Senior Circuit number two. But instead, to McGraw's horror, Barney Dreyfuss, the Pirates' owner, opted to play against Ban Johnson's upstart champions, the Boston Americans, in what was termed "the championship of the United States." To make matters worse, not only did Pittsburgh lower itself to consort with the American League, but Boston won the best-of-nine showdown, five-to-three.

This made McGraw look all the more foolish the next year when, as early as July, with the Giants winging toward the National League pennant, Muggsy began to make declarations that he had no intention of meeting the American League champions should the Giants win. "I know the American League and its methods," he orated. "I ought to, for I paid for my knowledge. . . . They still have my money. . . . No one, not even my bitterest enemy ever accused me of being a fool."

Brush backed him to the hilt. "There is nothing in the constitution or playing rules of the National League, which requires the victorious club to submit its championship honors to a contest with a victorious club in a minor league," he declared.

Hardly another soul, however, agreed with the Giants' owner and manager. Mostly they were lambasted, simply, as "cowards" — all the more so as they were putting up the best record in either league. McGraw's team won 106 games, finishing 13 games ahead of the Cubs. Mathewson went 33–12 with a 2.03 earned run average, but even he had to take a backseat this year to the Iron Man, for McGinnity had his best season, going 35–8, 1.61. Dummy Taylor won 21 games and southpaw Hooks Wiltse 13, so the starting rotation won all but four of the 106 victories between them. McGraw had always been leery of left-handed pitchers, but now that more and more left-handed batters were coming into baseball, he saw the advantage of countering them with left-handed pitchers. And wouldn't you know it? Around the middle of the season, to add punch to his outfield, McGraw got Turkey Mike Donlin back, from Cincinnati, where he'd worn out his welcome by drinking and fighting. Donlin was soon even more of a presence in New York nightlife than McGraw. Lock up the showgirls!

The Giants' refusal to play the American League winner took on even more opprobrium because no less than the Highlanders were making a run at the American League pennant. McGraw's old Baltimore buddy, Wee Willie Keeler, was the Highlanders' top hitter, and a spitballer named Jack Chesbro, who had kangarooed out of the National League, won forty-one games (still the modern record). In the event, the Highlanders finished a game and a half behind Boston and wouldn't do so well again until they were the Yankees, with Babe Ruth, in 1920, but the possibility of playing — and losing to! — the nouveau Manhattan opposition — the Old Oriole franchise itself — obviously gnawed at McGraw.

He protested that he was only taking the high road. "We are not a lot of grafters looking for box-office receipts at the expense of our club," he brayed sanctimoniously. Nobody fell for that hooey, least of all his players, who were furious that they were being cheated out of a terrific payday. Under McGraw's urging, Brush had, for his heroes, built a new state-of-the-art twentieth-century locker room, complete with electricity and steam heat, but the players knew that Brush was cleaning up off their popularity. Indeed, the Giants, with the Polo Grounds capacity expanded to twenty-four thousand, drew an incredible season's attendance of half a million, giving Brush a profit of one hundred thousand dollars — an unheard-of figure at that time.

But despite all the criticism, the Giants refused to play Boston. Brush, however, didn't possess McGraw's thick skin, and during the off-season he relented for the future, chairing the commission that laid out rules for what would, in 1905 and thereafter, first be known as the World's Championship Series, and then the World's Series, and then the World Series, and then the Series between the two major league pennant winners. Effectively, that was the last clause in the peace pact between the leagues. Only John J. McGraw continued to carry a grudge.

Of course, Muggsy loved playing the villain. With the possible exception of, fifty years on, the Boston Celtics' Red Auerbach smugly lighting up a huge victory cigar, no American coach or manager ever succeeded in so antagonizing rival players and fans. He was unrepentant. He went out of his way. After the Giants won the World Series in 1905, he actually had world's champions stitched not only on his players' shirt fronts, but also on the huge yellow blankets thrown over the horses that pulled the tally-hos the Giants traveled in from their road hotels, where they dressed, to the ballparks.

Talk about asking for it.

In Brooklyn, at Washington Park, fans began to throw spears fashioned out of umbrella tips at the Giant outfielders. Outside the parks, thugs lay in wait for the hated New Yorks. In Philadelphia particularly, the Giants themselves had to stock up on rocks, the better to return the fire of angry fans who bombarded their carriages. In Pittsburgh, the journey from hotel to ballyard took the Giants past a large produce market, so that along with the usual complement of gravel and bricks that the citizens of the Steel City hurled at the Giants, the players also had to duck a barrage of fruits and vegetables. Apparently, cost being no object when it came to attacking Muggsy McGraw's satanic team, even cantaloupes were employed as ammunition. On one occasion in Pittsburgh, a woman turned a strong hose on the Giants. McGraw only added fuel to the fire by urging his charges to, mockingly, scream out the names of the proprietors who were listed on the signs of stores. Often McGraw would wire ahead to the next city the Giants were visiting, requesting police protection, a publicized ploy, which, of course, only encouraged the need for more police protection. It all added to the fun, he chuckled, like "the spirit of skylarking college boys."

Yet the antagonistic Giant spirit, it seems, occasionally caught up even the exemplary Mathewson. To the dismay of fans across the Republic who had already come to worship Matty for his sportsmanlike demeanor, a near riot at a game in Philadelphia in April of 1905 culminated with a rare show of aggression from Mathewson. In the melee, he was accused of knocking down a boy — a boy! — who was selling lemonade near the Giants' bench, splitting the lad's lip and loosening several of his teeth. A dismayed letter-writer to the *Sporting News* moaned that this sorry incident showed that it was impossible for anyone connected with McGraw to escape his evil ways, that the dreadful assault was "just to show that his association with the old Baltimore crowd had made a hoodlum out of [even Christy Mathewson]."

On the field, McGraw remained as cantankerous as ever. He was the laird of the realm. In 1905, Harry Pulliam, the National League president, suspended McGraw for fifteen games for brawling with the Pittsburgh manager, Fred Clarke, and screaming obscenities at the Pittsburgh owner, Barney Dreyfuss. McGraw always took a special ornery delight in tormenting Pulliam, whom he called "the boy president," so he was especially pleased when he obtained an injunction in civil court against his suspension, and then was exonerated by the league's Board of Directors.

Then the next year, in the midst of the 1906 pennant race against Chicago, on August 6 at the Polo Grounds, McGraw protested a call by umpire James Johnstone so vociferously and profanely that he was evicted. Harry Steinfeldt, the Cubs third baseman, overheard the tirade and "reluctantly" wrote an account of the incident when Pulliam requested it. It's one of the more interesting documents on file at the Hall of Fame, Steinfeldt testifying that he heard McGraw call Johnstone "a damn dirty cock eating bastard, and a low-lived son-of-a-bitch of a yellow cur hound." It provides us with the one verifiable account we have of the sort of language McGraw evidently regularly employed.

Steinfeldt also wrote that McGraw had added "that if he had anything to do with it, Johnstone would never come into the Polo Grounds again." Sure enough, when Johnstone showed up to officiate the next day's game, he was barred at the gate. When the other umpire, Bob Emslie, heard this, he promptly departed the premises. McGraw then tried to talk Frank Chance, the so-called Peerless Leader of the Cubs, into having a substitute from each club umpire that day's contest. Chance would have none of that, and so, naturally, the game was forfeited to the Cubs.

The eleven thousand fans who had traveled to the Polo Grounds were, of course, furious, so when Johnstone showed up the next day, he got perhaps the only standing ovation ever accorded an umpire in major league annals. The fans "cheered him until they were hoarse." Writing in the *Washington Post*, J. T. Kelly described pretty much what the rest of the baseball world thought about Muggsy's "baby tactics" that so infuriated the paying customers. "McGraw can't fail but read the finger marks on the wall," the columnist wrote. "Too long has McGraw abused the patience of the hoi polloi. . . . The trick was irretrievably rotten, and all the perfumes of

Arabia will not nullify the stench. . . . McGraw has a host of admirers who gloried in his aggressive and successful tactics. A scrappy, fighting leader is always admired, but when a manager stoops to a contemptible trick, such as Tuesday's black eye to the national sport, it is high time to call a halt."

Using words like "blackguardism," "jobbery," and "bulldozing," Pulliam suspended McGraw for three games. The president was so furious that he threatened to "quit professional baseball forever" if his decision should be overruled by the league's Board of Directors — as had his earlier ruling against McGraw. If this penalty improved Muggsy's behavior, however, no one was aware of it. Poor, bedraggled President Pulliam vowed to eradicate "the brand of sportsmanship known as 'McGrawism.'" But who was listening? Muggsy seemed only to grow in stature, and in the eyes of his players, with each explosive episode. "There's only been one manager," said Connie Mack, "and his name is John McGraw."

Crowed, most famously, the infielder "Laughing Larry" Doyle: "It's great to be young and a Giant."

TWELVE

The World Series of 1905 was the first that was officially set in place as a postseason event, anxiously anticipated by sports fans across the nation. The two leagues were at peace, accepted as equals, while the Giants were almost indisputably acclaimed the preeminent team in the majors. They had, after all, won 106 and 105 games in successive years; they drew the largest crowds, home and away, engendering the most passion; they represented the largest city in the country; they were managed by the most controversial and famous man in the game . . . and now, on top of all this, as the season progressed, Christy Mathewson began to emerge, definitively, as the most popular player. Perhaps never has an athlete had such a rendezvous with a championship. Certainly none has ever embraced fate so well. Two days before the Series began, the redoubtable Dan Patch, astounding the nation, broke his own record by pacing a mile in 1:55.2. Within a week Matty had exceeded even those equine heroics, to become the most celebrated creature in the land.

The World's Championship Series might have still been referred to modestly as the Inter-League Series by a few cautious observers who refused to be wrapped in the hype, but the wiser students caught on fairly quickly that here was a divertissement that captured America's fancy quite unlike anything else before. Ring Lardner got it. "The World Serious," he would tab it.

Well, what else had there been? Oh, Barnum had rolled out his freaks and brought the "Swedish Nightingale," Jenny Lind, to these innocent shores; Philadelphia had presented the U.S. Centennial; and then Chicago had the Columbian Exposition, which gave us the Ferris wheel, and Cracker Jack, too. And yes, even the presidential campaign of '92 had been sidetracked when, in New Orleans, the "Boston Strong Boy," the Great John L. Sullivan, fought the "California Dude," Gentleman Jim Corbett, a/k/a "Pompadour Jim." Until that time, Western Union had never had such a night. As the *Boston Post* rhymed:

Lo! All the country held its breath
To hear the wired blows;
And strong men trembled pale as death,
When Corbett broke John's nose.
Oh! Sullivan the mighty fell —
The champion's fate was grim,
But as for Jimmy Corbett — well,
THERE ARE NO FLIES ON HIM!

Still, for all the attention that those two gladiators received in '92, the sweet science, so called, lacked the universal approval of the American national sport. Indeed, boxing was still outlawed in most of the forty-four states. The additional fact that, for goodness sake, it was just two Micks punching each other silly further diminished interest in many quarters of the Republic. But — aha! — the Series of ought-five had no flies on it. The handsome, elegant, educated Mathewson's rise to glory only added to the splendor.

It was this season when Matty eclipsed all the competition. At the age of twenty-four, he was 31–9 with thirty-one complete games, eight shutouts, and an earned run average of 1.28. His control was such that he handed out only about two walks every nine innings while also leading the league in strikeouts. He tossed his second no-hitter in June in Chicago. This year, no pitcher in either league — not his teammate the Iron Man nor his uptown spitball rival Jack Chesbro — approached him. With the wider plate and the changed rules that counted fouls as strikes, pitchers generally dominated. Moreover, pitchers, like Mathewson, were simply getting taller and stronger; Matty himself was six-feet-two, 195. Really, the bountiful hitting statistics of the Gay Nineties did not reappear again until the ball was hopped up for the Roaring Twenties. Pitchers were the glamour-pusses of this era.

Certainly, it also helped Mathewson's popular stature that there was no great offensive player who was a matinee idol. McGraw's Old Oriole teammates were over the hill. The contemporary batter with the highest lifetime average in the game, .346, Ed Delahanty, had died under mysterious circumstances in the middle of the 1903 season, when somehow — almost surely in his cups — he was put off a train and then fell off a bridge at Niagara Falls and drowned. In 1905, Ty Cobb was a rookie hitting .240. Tris Speaker and "Shoeless Joe" Jackson had yet to arrive in the majors. Larry Lajoie and Honus Wagner were the two most established hitting superstars, and while they were well liked within the game, both were ethnic minorities and not very marketable. Larry was French-Canadian, the ungainly Honus of German heritage.

McGraw went to his grave maintaining that Wagner was the best player he ever saw. Of course, there might have been an ulterior motive in this declaration. It always galled McGraw that Babe Ruth — a Baltimore boy, no less — would come to New York and steal the Giants' thunder. "Why shouldn't we pitch to Ruth?" McGraw asked with false bravado in 1921, when the Giants first faced the Yankees in a World Series. "We've pitched to better hitters in the National League."

As for Cobb, he and McGraw were probably too much of the same pugnacious temperament ever to be able to appreciate each other, but as it was, they truly found each other despicable. Indeed, Mathewson may have been the only rival the misanthropic Cobb ever liked. "Matty was a hero of mine," the "Georgia Peach" said. "He was truly magnificent in every way — no other phrase fits." But McGraw? After Cobb took on one of McGraw's players, Buck Herzog, in a hotel fight, pummeling Herzog near to a pulp, McGraw sought out

Cobb. Perhaps luckily for McGraw, who was fat and out of shape by this time, Cobb only called him a "mucker," threatening to kill him if he were younger. Only years later when a mutual friend was dying did McGraw and Cobb deign to make up out of tribute to the old player they both loved. The player on his deathbed would be, of course, Mathewson.

Wagner, a shortstop who would scoop up great globs of dirt with his giant hands as he gobbled up grounders, was an absolutely magnificent player, a .327 hitter lifetime, the only infielder to make the first class of the Hall of Fame — with Mathewson, Cobb, Ruth, and Walter Johnson. But he was an unattractive fellow, jug-eared and heavy-set, and though Wagner spoke unaccented English, he was never really thought of as a mainstream figure. Like so many German-Americans, he was called "Dutch" (from "Deutsch") and was known as the "Flying Dutchman," and remained more of a German immigrant hero. It would be another generation before a player of German descent — the one named George Herman Ruth — could qualify as a full-fledged American idol.

So Mathewson came to achieve unsurpassed popularity, and for the Giants' first

Series game, McGraw naturally chose him as his starter. Back then, when the two teams playing were geographically close, a coin was flipped to determine who got the inaugural honor, and then home games were simply alternated (although rainouts could change this routine somewhat). In 1905, Philadelphia won the flip. Rather than spend the night on the road, though, the Giants preferred to commute, taking the train down in the morning, then returning to their hearths and homes immediately following each away game.

Indeed, the night before the opener in Philadelphia, most of the Giants gathered on Broadway, attending a gala in their honor, which was graced by the presence of many show business celebrities, who were "dyed in the wool supporters themselves." Naturally, DeWolf Hopper was the star, and when he appeared — surprise, surprise — "the entire audience . . . demanded 'Casey at the Bat.' " First, though, acting as something of a surrogate for his pal Muggsy, Hopper addressed the fawning crowd. "Owing to the arduous week which is before the Giants," he orated, "Manager McGraw has deemed it wise to send some of the players home to get a good night's rest. Early to bed and plenty of removal from the excitement are two things which are necessary before a world's series championship."

As the " 'bleacherites' in the gallery yelled themselves hoarse," Matty and many of the regulars thereupon departed to join the sandman. Hopper then brought McGraw up on stage, and although reports did not indicate exactly what he said, we are assured by the *Herald*'s reporter that he was "much more friendly than he addresses the umpires." Only then did Hopper bring down the house with the "Ballad of the Republic."

On to the City of Brotherly Love!

The Athletics had lost the services of their ace, left-hander Rube Waddell, who, with a 27–10 record, had been the closest thing to Matty in the American League. Reportedly, Waddell had injured his pitching shoulder monkeying around with some of his teammates, but many observers took a much darker view of his injury. Almost from its first, baseball had been a popular gambling game. The fixed World Series of 1919 was a climax rather than an oddity. So on this occasion there was a natural suspicion — indeed, almost an assumption — that gamblers must have gotten to Waddell and paid him to come down with a convenient injury that would take him out of the Series and reward those who then had bet the Giants before the news got out.

Notwithstanding, a great deal of anti-Giant money poured into Philadelphia, especially from Boston and Pittsburgh. At the Continental Hotel, Giants headquarters, the *World* reported that "fistfuls of money were waved about the hotel corridors with as much abandon as if they had been cabbage leaves." The *Sun* predicted that "even money will probably prevail if the Quaker is as fine with his coin as the Knickerbocker."

The Quaker was not, however, and the line favoring the Giants moved up to 10–9, then to 5–4. Even then, with Waddell out, that seemed like an overlay. Still, McGraw himself bet four hundred dollars on his team at even money, and many of his players followed his lead. (There are no reports whether Matty got down.) On the other hand, many of the Giants paired up with A's players and agreed to an even split in the prize money no matter which team won. The pot was set by the two leagues, with 75 percent of the players' share earmarked to the winners, but players on both teams matched up so they'd be guaranteed a 50 percent share regardless of the outcome. This was not considered ethically untoward, but McGraw was furious, fuming that you could be damn sure his Old Orioles never played it safe. "I was disgusted at their unwillingness to take a chance," he declared.

Off to the lidlifter!

Days of the week in the United States were then designated for the appointed household chores. This October 9 was a Monday — Washing Day. The Athletics' park was in a section of Philadelphia known as Brewerytown, and indeed, the pungent beermaking odors wafted o'er an SRO crowd of 17,955 that came out on a cool, early autumn day. Everybody wore hats in America then. Photographs of crowds, such as at a ballpark, show literally hundreds of men, not so much as a single one of them bareheaded. The only difference would be that derbies were worn in the winter, straw boaters in summer. This Washing Day was one strictly for derbies.

And the men of Philadelphia were primed to pour out their venom upon Mathewson. Remember, he'd busted up the little lemonade vendor right here, back in April. The bleachers were enclosed with chicken wire to keep the more boisterous fans trapped within. But, oh, did they get an eyeful when the Giants took the field. McGraw had outfitted his men in brand-spanking-new uniforms — basic black with only a white NY insignia, plus white belts, socks, and cap beaks. "The effect of being togged out in snappy uniforms was immediately noticeable among the players," one New York reporter gloated. "The Athletics appeared dull alongside our players."

About five hundred New Yorkers made the trip down, and although, midst the Philadelphia throng, they were "like a peanut in a bushel basket," they cheered wildly for their ebony-garbed heroes, and when Gotham's fifty-six-piece Catholic prefectory band struck up "Give My Regards to Broadway," George M. Cohan himself led the rousing song. Pompadour Jim Corbett was such a Giant fixture that he worked out with the team before the game, and then he and Roger Bresnahan, the tempestuous catcher, waved a large Irish flag.

The A's had a little surprise, too. McGraw, remember, had some years before sought to disparage them as "white elephants." This had, however, become something of a badge of honor for the team, and the A's had taken to wearing little elephant logos on their warm-up sweaters. Now, just before the game started, Connie Mack, the tall, gaunt Philadelphia manager, who eschewed a baseball uniform for a business suit (complete with high collar and stickpin), called McGraw to home plate and presented him with a small, carved white elephant. Muggsy thereupon delighted the crowd by doffing his white-beaked cap, making a sweeping bow, and then dancing an Irish jig.

Play ball!

The A's sent that star collegian of their own, Eddie Plank, to the mound. A southpaw, Plank had won twenty-four games during this season and been almost as dominating as the absent Waddell. True to form, Plank got the Giants out in the first inning, beginning what would probably be the most sustained domination of pitching ever seen in baseball, let alone in a World Series. For the five games, only six pitchers were used. All five games were shutouts, with both teams combining to score a total of only eight earned runs in eighty-eight innings at bat.

Even in this brilliant company, though, Mathewson was the nonpareil. He retired the side in the first inning on five pitches, a fair sample of all that followed when he was on the mound. In the fifth inning, Mathewson was clobbered by a line drive hit by outfielder Socks Seybold, stung so hard in the thigh that after Matty retrieved the carom and tossed the batter out, he had to repair to the bench. But after the leg was inspected and he deemed himself fit enough, he returned to the mound and shut out the A's the rest of the way on four hits. The Giants won 3–0. "Matty is certainly a phenomenon," McGraw said.

The Giants returned home for the first World Series game ever contested in New York, and the stadium was overflowing this Tuesday — Ironing Day. The mob poured onto the field before the game. Attendance was announced at 25,000, but the players and other cynical observers suspected that it might have been as much as 30,000, that the Giants' management was lowballing the figure to keep down the players' share of the gate. In any event, the *Herald* found the crowd to be "full of American health, vigor and optimistic enthusiasm." References to baseball then were invariably larded with favorable qualities that, often as not, were employed to also reflect on the best of all America.

But, alas, for the joyful throng, Chief

Bender — "the much favored brave," as the *Times* described him — matched Matty's four-hitter from the day before. The A's won by the identical 3–0 score, besting McGinnity. One game apiece.

Returning to Philadelphia, the third game, on Wednesday, October 11, Sewing Day, was rained out, so even though Thursday, Market Day, came up raw and cold, McGraw decided to bring back Mathewson to officiate on but two days' rest. Only 10,991 ventured over to Brewerytown to see Andy Coakley, another of Mr. Mack's collegians — from Holy Cross — toe the rubber for the A's. It was not pretty for the home side. Coakley gave up nine hits but, behind him, his team made four errors, and the Giants coasted to a second victory, 9–0. Once again, Mathewson allowed only four hits.

New Yorkers were able to follow the game on large billboards that some newspapers set up outside their offices. As the reports came in by telegraph, the news would be relayed by a man with a megaphone, while on a large, simulated diamond, player figures would be moved about the bases. Next, though, the real players returned to Manhattan and, out at the Polo Grounds, on Friday the thirteenth, Cleaning Day, it was Iron Man's turn to shut out the A's. He beat the luckless Eddie Plank, 1–0. "Goose eggs are becoming as staple an item of Father Penn's diet as scrapple," the *Sun* crowed.

Because of the rain-out, the fifth game was also scheduled for New York. It was easily the grandest sports day in the history of any American city. Not only was there the World Series, but out on Long Island, one of the first major automobile races, the Vanderbilt Cup, was being contested. It drew crowds in excess of one hundred thousand, including many anxious members of Mrs. Astor's famous Four Hundred. SOCIETY LOSES SLEEP, BUT SEES THE THRILLING RACE, headlined the *Herald*. Even the most blasé New Yorkers had to be astounded by the speed, as the winner was timed at 61.5 miles per hour — "hurtling over the oil soaked course at a rate of speed which can only be likened to that of the wind," *Tribune* readers were advised.

Notwithstanding this gasoline-powered marvel of modern times, Matty was just as impressive at his game with his soupbone. In the *Herald*, a poem signed by Diedrich Knickerbocker put things in perspective for true New Yorkers:

193

Let others sing of motor cars,
Extol the record run;
But let me sing, oh Stripes and Stars,
Of Christy Mathewson.

The crowd overflowed the Polo Grounds, reaching perhaps 27,000, as fans stood ten-deep behind the outfield ropes. It was a pretty day, and a spirited throng came to celebrate the championship. "Clinch it today," they called out to McGraw.

"That's what you'll get," Muggsy hollered back. Then, when that "Argus-eyed" manager saw Chief Bender, "that stolid, phlegmatic, copper-colored man" who was Matty's pitching opponent this afternoon, McGraw had some sprightly new Indian-tuned badinage for him. "It'll be off the warpath for you today, Chief," he hee-hawed.

Not to be outdone, Turkey Mike Donlin sallied: "I'm sorry, old Pitch-Em-Heap, but here's where you go back to the reservation."

With Matty on the mound, the Giants were obviously confident and in high spirits.

And yes, now here comes a-tootin' that Giant big-game staple, the Catholic prefectory band. Today's choice offerings were "Johnny Comes Marching Home," "Carry the News to Mary," and the Tammany Hall fight song. That brought down the house: *Tamm . . . annn . . . eeeee!*

Then Matty took off his duster and, once again, began to toy with the A's. They did manage all of five hits and actually got one man to second base, but Mathewson shut them out again. Bender himself permitted only five hits, but the Giants got one run in the fifth without making a hit, and Matty himself scored in the eighth when he walked, went to third when Bresnahan knocked a ground-rule double into the crowd, and then scored on an infield smash.

The whole affair took barely an hour and a half, and when Matty got the last out with a ground out, New York's finest were overwhelmed, unable to halt the joyous mob from pouring onto the field. Somehow, Matty and Muggsy and the other Giants found their way to the safety of their center-field clubhouse.

As the crowd surged after the Giants, naturally the name most cheered was Mathewson. Never since has any pitcher — any player — dominated a World Series as Matty did. He had pitched three shutouts in six days, allowing only fourteen hits and a single walk. He struck out eighteen batters and, never mind score, he allowed but one Athletic to reach third base. The *Times* was especially beside itself, calling his a "superhuman accomplishment," adding: "The Giant slabman . . . may legitimately be designated as the premier pitching wonder. . . . [Mathewson] bestrode the field like a mighty Colossus, and the Athletics peeped about the diamond like pigmies."

Over time, even Matty acknowledged that it was the best he ever officiated.

Out in center field, one by one the Giants ventured onto the pavilion to greet their worshipers below. Some of them even tossed their gloves and caps into the happy mob. A pretty debutante was heard to sigh: "I'd like one of those old gloves to put among my cotillion favors." But no matter how many of the victors showed themselves, it was Mathewson the crowd wanted.

Finally, he not only appeared, but he and Bresnahan unfurled a large banner, hurriedly made up, that read:

THE GIANTS
WORLD'S CHAMPIONS 1905

That produced "a reverberating roar that lifted Manhattan's soil from the base." In all of New York's history, there had never been a moment like this. Why, this was New York's first secular communion. If not already the first city of the world, it would pass London and Paris soon enough. Anyway, it was already a depot of dreams, and what could have certified that more than this triumph at the American national sport?

"Big Six" waited for the tumult to die down, and then he was his proper, modest Mathewsonian self. "Gentlemen," he said, "I want to thank you for your kindness, but you must remember there were eight other members of the team who worked for our success just as much as I did." That only occasioned more cheers to roll up to him, and then on to the heavens above. Saith the *Times*, which now put baseball on the front page: "Baseball New York gave Mathewson a marvelous vocal panegyric and placed upon his modest brow a billowed wreath that evoked only a half-suppressed smile and bow."

Only one more Giant did the crowd call for. And finally here he came, McGraw emerging to address the multitude. As befits a Napoleon, his speech, as it often was when he was neither at the bar nor upon the field of play, was courtly. "Ladies and gentlemen," Muggsy proclaimed solemnly, "I appreciate the great victory as well as you. I thank you for your patronage and hope to see you all next spring."

So he would. But who would have ever imagined that it would never again be the same for Matty and Muggsy as it was on this one most glorious of all Baking Days.

THIRTEEN

By 1912 the *Literary Digest* would write: "The name of Christy Mathewson . . . is known to about as many people as that of any man in the United States except President Taft, Colonel Roosevelt and William Jennings Bryan." Inasmuch as Roosevelt had been president before Taft and Bryan had run for the office three times, that shows what kind of popular company the pitcher was in. Not only that, but for all his fame, Matty's personal reputation remained impeccable. Ray Robinson, Mathewson's biographer, writes: "It is a safe prediction that no sports figure will ever again approach the hold that Matty once had on America in the early days of the new twentieth century."

In a sense, Mathewson had it both ways. The public thought he was faultless, while those who knew him thought Matty was wonderfully human. Donald Honig, the sports historian, wrote: "He was the first truly national baseball figure who captured the country's admiration and hero worship by combining all the elements of baseball, religion and American culture. . . . In a broadly 'religious sense,' he epitomized humanity as it was created in the Garden of Eden. He lived and played in a 'garden paradise,' a pure specimen of the ideal ballplayer and created being." Not surprisingly, Honig felt that Mathewson was such a paragon that he lifted the whole sport of "baseball's pure, idyllic status" to a higher level.

Yet if Mathewson was somewhat distant from most of his fellow ballplayers, they liked him a great deal. On his own terms, Mathewson was a regular guy. How else could he get along so well with McGraw? In the term of that time, he was no "prig." Said Laughing Larry Doyle: "We were a rough, tough lot in those days. All except Matty. But he was no namby-pamby. He'd gamble, play cards, curse now and then and take a drink now and then. But he was always quiet and had a lot of dignity. I remember how fans would constantly rush up to him and pester him with questions. He hated it, but he was always courteous. I never saw a man who could shake off those bugs so slick without hurting their feelings."

By the same token, Mathewson would pull down the shades in his sleeping car so that he would be protected from the view of fans who came out to the station specifically to catch a glimpse of him. He drew a firm line in these matters. "I owe everything I have to the fans when I'm out there on the mound," he declared, "but I owe the fans nothing and they owe me nothing when I'm not pitching."

When the city of New York gave its first baseball parade in honor of the 1905 champions the next June 12, Mathewson seems to have smiled down almost beatifically upon the worshipers who lined the great route that went from Union Square to city hall. He was placed in the only white automobile — with McGraw and Turkey Mike Donlin — in the cavalcade that included all the Giants (plus those old reliables DeWolf Hopper and Gentleman Jim Corbett). He was well recovered from his spring's bout with diphtheria by now, and he greeted his fans jauntily, "his arm flung with careful carelessness over the back of the automobile."

As the *Times* reported, "Big Six" was the cynosure. " 'Hooray for Matty,' yelled a dirty little street arab.

" 'Who is that they are cheering?' asked

a man who was caught in the crowd.

" 'Aw, doncher know Matty?' asked the boy in tones full of disgust."

On the mound, Mathewson would brush back batters and occasionally even argue with umpires. Never, though, was there any trash-talking to the hitters he faced; he left that to McGraw. "Repartee is not my line," Matty said. But neither did he take any guff from Muggsy. There's a story told by Jimmy McAleer, a contemporary manager of the St. Louis Browns, about how McGraw would let Mathewson position his outfielders — a responsibility he denied all his other pitchers. In a key game, Muggsy suddenly decided to regain that power. He signaled to the outfielders to shift their spacing. They followed his command. Mathewson glared at McGraw, then turned around and tried to reposition the outfielders as he desired them. The poor outfielders, in McGraw's thrall, wouldn't budge. Mathewson glowered at McGraw, then simply reared back and struck out the side, not allowing anyone to hit a ball to McGraw's outfield. Muggsy got the point. He didn't want Mathewson just firing for strikeouts. He immediately resumed his old practice of letting Matty position his outfielders his way.

It didn't hurt Mathewson's image that he was also exceptionally handsome. His countenance was friendly and kind and touched with sympathy. He parted his wavy brown hair in the middle and filled out a suit nicely. Altogether, he was the exemplar of the Gibson Man, that fresh-faced, well-groomed, broad-shouldered, quintessentially turn-of-the-century American male. Who knows how many young men stopped wearing mustaches because Matty was clean-shaven? Women would send him mash notes (which Jane would politely answer). One contemporary summed up Mathewson this way: "He talks like a Harvard graduate, looks like an actor, acts like a businessman and impresses you as an all-around gentleman."

He read seriously and regularly, taking such works as those by Victor Hugo, William James, and Charles Lamb on the road with him. Horticulture interested him. He played golf in the low seventies and was superb at cards. Heywood Broun, the journalist, was Matty's regular partner at bridge and whist. He was also a ruthless poker player and accomplished at chess. Mathewson's best game, though, was checkers. At one point he was elected second vice president of the American

Checkers Association. Mathewson would take on all comers, playing up to half a dozen games simultaneously. He could even play blindfolded, because he had numbered the board in his own mind and needed to be told only where the checkers were. Regularly, whenever he would lose two or three games on the mound, some critic would write that Mathewson was wasting his concentration on checkers. McGraw, though, would never have any of that. On the contrary, he took great pride in that a baseball player could be so good at a game of the mind. Muggsy would even often take Mathewson over to the Lambs Club to, in effect, show him off beating everyone at checkers.

If Matty had any physical defect, it was his unusually high voice. (One thinks of Jack Nicklaus or Mike Tyson, who also have voices that don't seem deep enough for their big, athletic bodies.) So a few of his detractors did call him "Sis." He was also known as "Old Gumboots" for his slightly knock-kneed gait. But that was about as critical as anybody could get of Christy Mathewson. Well, Damon Runyon thought he was a bit much when Matty told him: "I think any man who cheats on his wife would betray his country."

The comparison with the fictional Frank Merriwell was a common one. In fact, so closely was Matty identified with that make-believe idol that Edward Stratemeyer, a children's books producer who would also develop the Hardy Boys and Nancy Drew thrillers, took advantage of Mathewson's hero status to create a character named "Baseball Joe." Stratemeyer had no shame; Baseball Joe was almost indecently drawn from Mathewson. Writing under the pseudonym Lester Chadwick, Stratemeyer wrote at least fourteen Baseball Joe books.

Our hero, Joe Matson, resided in the bucolic town of Riverside, where he lived an exemplary life; indeed, art followed life so closely that Momsey wanted him to be a minister. But Joe was just too good at baseball. From prep school at Excelsior Hall, Joe proceeded to Yale (just like Merriwell), and then, in *On the Giants*, he went on to play in New York for Manager McRae (hmm). It was a busy time for Baseball Joe, as he knocked out a kidnapper with an iceball and then saved his chaste girlfriend Mabel by hurling a stone at a leopard that was menacing her. (Never mind how the great jungle cat got to Riverside.) Then came the real good news. "The Giants,

Sis!" Joe hollered, opening a letter from Manager McRae. "The class of the National League. I'm getting right to the top of the ladder. I'm going to play with the first team in the biggest city in the most famous grounds in the United States!"

Whether or not Mathewson thought he was being ripped off, he then got into the game himself. Working with a writer named John Wheeler, Matty began turning out children's novels. Wheeler always maintained that he really only edited Mathewson's work. Anyway, Mathewson was given full credit, thusly:

By CHRISTY MATHEWSON ("Matty")

These books were pretty juvenile, written for a somewhat younger crowd than the Baseball Joe series. They bear such titles as *Pitcher Pollock, Catcher Craig, First Baseman Faulkner.* You get the idea. Tom Pollock, for example, is a bashful, redheaded orphan with a faithful dog named Star, who lives alone in Amesville, Ohio (pop. 25,000), where he works in a hardware store and "in high school, was a person of prominence." Tom certainly does not have a girlfriend because "pretty young ladies were things he had little to do with." Whew. But, of course, Tom wins the big game against Petersburg with the same guile as Matty.

"Arm getting tired?" asks the coach.

"No, sir, it's my head. I never knew before that a pitcher did so much pitching with his head."

"Bully work, Pollock!"

So, however much Wheeler might have contributed, Mathewson did use his books to justify his own career and air his beliefs. In *Second Baseman Sloan*, for example, the hero is assured that "you can be a baseball player and a gentleman, too."

Matty also wrote his own memoir, *Pitching in a Pinch*, which was a fairly good seller; it even had a special Boy Scout edition. ("Pinch" at that time was something of a synonym for "crisis." McGraw pretty much invented the position and the term "pinch hitter" by regularly using a reserve named Sammy Strang in that capacity.) Touching all the bases, Mathewson also was credited with coauthoring a Broadway play in 1913 with one Rida Johnson Young. It was entitled *The Girl and the Pennant*. The plot concerns a young woman who inherits her father's baseball club, and then falls in love with the pitcher who wins the big game. It was, however, something

less than a hit, closing after twenty perfor-
mances.

At that time it was not unusual for baseball players to work in vaudeville in the off-
season. After all, professional athletes and
entertainers were held in the same dubious
regard. So it was that after the 1910
season, Matty and his catcher, Chief
Meyers, performed for seventeen weeks in
a sketch written by a sportswriter,
Bozeman Bulger, that was called "Curves,
1910." At a time when Mathewson was
probably the highest-paid player in the
game, earning $10,000 a season, he made
far more in vaudeville, cashing in at $1,000
a week. But as much as Matty liked money,
he was too shy on stage — remember:
"Repartee is not my line" — and so he did
not return to vaudeville in subsequent seasons. Matty did, however, perform in several one-reel films, with such titles as
Breaking into the Big Leagues, *The Umpire*,
and *Love and Baseball.*

He also became pretty much of a match
for Dan Patch in the endorsement field.
He lent his name to razors, sweaters, a
parlor baseball game, Tuxedo pipe tobacco
("Tuxedo gets to me in a natural, pleasant
way"), and Coca-Cola (Matty's "proof of
its wholesomeness"). Mathewson also was

called upon to publicly assure Americans that he was going to buy more stocks after the market took something of a tumble, and he started his own insurance agency, but he drew the line at licensing a "drinking and dining place" to open under the name of The Christy Mathewson.

That made his mother happy. She had reluctantly come to accept the fact that her eldest wasn't going to become a preacher, but she had concluded that Matty did indeed have a ministry of sorts. "His work has brought him before the multitude in a kindly manner; his example is a cleanly one," Minerva Mathewson said. "He reaches the masses of the people in his own way, and he must give them something through his character."

Invariably, Matty was not just identified as a mere gentleman, but as a "Christian gentleman." This was a time when the United States could fairly be called a part of Christendom, and what was known as "muscular Christianity" had gained a respectable foothold, especially midst the prep school and college establishment. No one represented that concept better than Matty. "I feel strongly that it is my duty to show youth the good, clean, honest values that I was taught by my mother," he said.

"That, really, is all I can do."

He was even honored as one of the four famous muscular Christians that the sports bay in the Cathedral of St. John the Divine in upper Manhattan is dedicated to. The other three are from the Ivy League's trinity: Walter Camp of Yale, the godfather of football; Robert Wrenn of Harvard, an early U.S. tennis champion who was one of Teddy Roosevelt's Rough Riders; and Hobey Baker of Princeton, the first great American ice hockey player and an aviation hero of World War I, immortalized all the more in that he fell to his death in France. Significantly, too, Matty is the only professional athlete who is celebrated at the cathedral for his sportsmanship, in stained-glass windows that portray such athletic Biblical figures as Esau, Samson, and David.

Matty honored his mother by not pitching on Sundays where it was legal, in Chicago, St. Louis, and Cincinnati. This is not to say he wasn't torn on the issue, even as the Sabbath Society zealously fought to deny New Yorkers the sacrilege of watching baseball on the Lord's Day. (The Dodgers tried to get around the statutes by not selling tickets, only asking for contributions, but the constabulary eventually ended that scam.) In 1907, as doubleheaders piled up, Mathewson told McGraw that he could call on him on a Sunday if it was absolutely necessary. It wasn't. But eventually Mathewson came to sympathize with the workingman, who often was able to attend games only on Sundays, and by 1917, when he was managing Cincinnati, he and McGraw broke the law to play a benefit game on Sunday at the Polo Grounds for the war cause. Times were a-changing. The judge not only dismissed the Sabbath Society's charge, but praised Matty and Muggsy for their patriotism.

But it was not only a different day because of the war. Mathewson had himself brought about a change in the way America looked at athletes. For all of McGraw's proselytizing about how bright baseball players really were, his own demeanor always made it difficult for society to heed him. Mathewson, however, was Exhibit A. He certainly was the prime model who encouraged other more educated young men to try and make a living at baseball. (Coincidentally, Mathewson was not only the first famous American professional athlete to be identified with college, but he actually gets credit for coining perhaps the most famous popular expression *about* college. In 1919, writing an article in the *New York Times*, when he referred to the "Fordham Flash," Frankie Frisch, Mathewson wrote that Frisch "was taking a long hold on his club and the old college try at the ball." Nobody, it seems, had ever used the term "old college try" before.)

By the time World War I ended, nearly a fourth of all major leaguers had at least attended college. It's certainly true that it was Babe Ruth's heroics that, foremost, saved baseball at this point after the Black Sox scandal, but it's also for sure that because baseball rosters had begun to represent a more genteel cross section of society, it was easier for the public to forgive an institution with a more respectable cadre that upstanding people could relate to. Had it still been McGraw and his immigrant muckers, who would have wanted to save it? Mathewson's image of sweetness and light might have been overdone, but that did serve, in the process of deifying him personally, to uplift his whole profession. "Christy Mathewson," wrote Grantland Rice, the great sports troubadour, "is the only man I ever met who in spirit and inspiration was greater than his game."

Benjamin Rader, a prominent sports historian, suggests that by becoming a new kind of hero, Mathewson and the sports idols that followed him played a beneficial part in taking America into the complex new century. "Athletes as public heroes served a compensatory cultural function," he wrote. "They assisted the public in compensating for the passing of the traditional dream of success, the erosion of Victorian values and the feelings of individual powerlessness. As the society became more complicated and as success had to be won increasingly in bureaucracies, the need for heroes who leapt to fame and fortune outside of the system seemed to grow."

Funnily enough, John McGraw, if only instinctively, probably was the first person to understand what sort of larger role Mathewson might play in the sport beyond his eminent value to him as a slabman.

FOURTEEN

Perhaps the greatest loss to television, to the utter visualization of sport at the expense of imagination, is the disappearance of the nickname. Gone, all gone. We're lucky now if a player is known by his number or his initials. That counts for originality. *Yo, Twelve. Yeah, M. J.* Oh, to be sure, there's the odd exception, but Willie Mays and Pete Rose were essentially the last baseball superstars with original sobriquets: the "Say-Hey Kid" and "Charlie Hustle." Well, Brooks Robinson had a title: the "Human Vacuum Cleaner." And pale as it was, at least "Hammerin'" Hank Aaron is something. But there's pretty slim pickins in the last half century after "Stan the Man," the "Yankee Clipper," and the "Splendid Splinter" retired.

Once Americans could see their heroes, there was no reason to embroider a name to further identify a player. Back when Muggsy and Matty played, though, most everybody was given some sort of nickname. Maybe it just related to his demeanor: "Turkey Mike." "Bad Bill" Dahlen. "Dirty Jack" Doyle. "Laughing Larry" Doyle. Bugs Raymond. "Cocky" Eddie Collins. Or some idiosyncrasy: "Shoeless Joe." "Iron Man." "Hooks." Geography: the "Georgia Peach." "Wahoo Sam" Crawford. "Gettysburg Eddie" Plank. Heritage: All those Chiefs and Dutches. "Harvard Eddie" Grant. The "Duke of Tralee" (Roger Bresnahan). "The Trojan" (Johnny Evers — he from Troy, New York). Some spoke to class: the "Peerless Leader." "The Grey Eagle" (Tris Speaker). The "Big Train" (Walter Johnson). The "Sultan of Swat." "Home Run" Baker. "Prince Hal" Chase. Some derived from the physical: Wee Willie. "Reds" galore. So too "Bigs." And the "Dummys." "Three-Fingered" Brown. "Handsome Harry" Howell. When Buck Herzog first came up to the Giants, he was assumed to be Jewish. He explained: "You've got me wrong, boys. I'm as Dutch as sauerkraut." Soon enough, though, given his unfortunate proboscis, Herzog was called "Dick Nose" (if only amongst his fellows).

McGraw, of course, was celebrated as "the Little Napoleon," which despite its redundancy he naturally adored. For a while when he was younger, he was called "Mickey Face." For some reason, it appears that he accepted that, perhaps as a badge to his Irishness. But he recoiled at Muggsy, despised it with all the venom in his bile-filled body.

There are two accounts of where the name came from. One has it that there was a comic strip tramp named Muggsy in a Baltimore newspaper that reminded teammates of McGraw. The other is that an unsavory Baltimore ward boss was named Muggsy McGraw. When the smart aleck new *New Yorker* magazine profiled the mature Manager McGraw in 1925, it wrote: "He probably hates that nickname worse than any one thing in the world." Of course, they entitled the piece "Mister Muggsy."

As for Mathewson, early on he became known as "Big Six." Given the wide usage of the proud title, it's surprising that no one then ever pinned down the provenance of the name. It did not, of course, have anything to do with his uniform number, inasmuch as players did not wear any numerals until long after Matty had retired. Some have suggested, though, that the origin was almost as simple, that it was merely because Mathewson was such an overpowering six-footer-plus back when six feet was tall. Or maybe it came from a "peerless" automobile manufactured by the Matheson Motor Company that was colloquially referred to as "Big Six."

The even more favored explanation is that a banjo-hitting batter-turned-sportswriter named Sam Newhall Crane, who in his finest early sportswriterese had termed Mathewson a "flame-thrower," took it one step further and started calling him "Big Six" after a local horse-drawn volunteer fire department engine that could, it was said, outpump Niagara Falls. But why, pray, if Matty was a flamethrower, would you name him after an anti-flamethrower?

Then, in one obscure recollection, long after Mathewson was finished pitching, McGraw himself claimed that it was none other than he who had given Mathewson his esteemed cognomen. As he recalled, there was a Typographical Union Number 6 in New York, which won a big strike settlement, so that day in Cincinnati, when Muggsy was asked who was officiating, he piped up: "Let's put in Big Six."

It's hard to make the connection, but then, to give the devil his due, McGraw was pretty good at naming things that stuck. As we know, he insulted the Athletics by calling them "White Elephants," and they have that symbol to this day. Likewise, he's credited with tabbing the saloon in Havana "Sloppy Joe's," and his regular usage of inserting Sammy Strang to bat in the clutch in 1905 gave us "pinch hitter."

In '06, McGraw's Giants probably wouldn't have been any match for the Cubs even if Mathewson hadn't missed the first part of the season with diphtheria. Even so, he won twenty-two games, and New York won ninety-six, but even with that outstanding total, the Giants finished *twenty* games behind the Cubs, whose 116–36 record is still the best of the twentieth century (and beyond). At the end of the day, so good were the Cubs that it didn't even matter that McGraw gave one of those wins to Chicago with his forfeit, when he locked out the umpire he was mad at.

The Cubs won handily in 1907, too, piling up 107 victories. They were a marvelous fielding team, featuring the double play combination of Joe Tinker, Johnny Evers, and Frank Chance (he the "Peerless Leader," who also managed Chicago). At a time when poems were a staple of the sports pages and sportswriters were not afraid to use words like "gonfalon," the most famous sports rhyme ever was written by Franklin P. Adams in the *Evening Mail*, immortalizing the six-four-three double play:

These are the saddest of possible words —
   Tinker to Evers to Chance.
Trio of Bear Cubs and fleeter than birds —
   Tinker to Evers to Chance.
Thoughtlessly pricking our gonfalon bubble,
Making a Giant hit into a double,
Words that are weighty with nothing
    but trouble:
Tinker to Evers to Chance.

The Cubs also possessed one truly great pitcher, Mordecai Peter Centennial Brown, who was born, as you might imagine, in 1876 and was called "Three-Fingered" Brown because, when he was seven years old, he had stuck his hand in a corn shucker. He lost most of his index finger, and one other digit and his thumb were mangled, but professionally this turned out to be a blessing because his mutilated hand somehow helped him break off a curveball that Ty Cobb called

219

"the most devastating pitch I ever faced." It was certainly a match for Mathewson's fadeaway, and indeed, Three-Fingered was Matty's greatest rival. Why, in *This Side of Paradise*, F. Scott Fitzgerald's young Midwestern alter ego, Amory Blaine, "was interested in . . . whether Three-Fingered Brown was really a better pitcher than Christie [*sic*] Mathewson."

The last game Mathewson would pitch would be in 1916, when he agreed to return to the mound for a special engagement against Brown on Labor Day. In honor of this valedictory, both old-timers were presented with bouquets of American Beauty roses. Matty was thirty-six, Three-Fingered thirty-nine, and between them they gave up thirty-four hits and eighteen runs, but Mathewson (who made three hits himself) prevailed 10–8, for his 373rd victory.

In 1908, though, Matty was at the height of his powers, and Three-Fingered had a fabulous season, too: a 29–9 record with a 1.47 ERA. Mathewson, though, was even more magnificent. He was 37–11, 1.43; he completed thirty-four of forty-four starts, throwing a dozen shutouts. In 391 innings pitched, he struck out 285 men and walked only 42, barely one per nine innings. The Giants were improved at the bat this year, too, largely because Turkey Mike Donlin had returned after a hiatus in which he had devoted himself to traveling with his bride, Mabel Hite, a beautiful chanteuse. In 1908, though, Turkey Mike was on the wagon and so well behaved that McGraw even made him captain. He hit .334, drove in 106 runs, and kept the Giants in the pennant race. Not only did the Cubs fall back, but the Pirates also moved up in what turned out to be a three-team dogfight, as good a pennant race as ever there has been. The Giants drew 910,000 fans, a quarter of the league total, and a major league attendance record that lasted until 1920, when The Babe and the Yankees passed a million.

On September 23 the Giants and Cubs were only six percentage points apart, just ahead of the Pirates, when thirty thousand fans showed up at the Polo Grounds to watch Matty face off against the lefty Jack Pfiester, who, for his uncommon success against New York, was known as Jack "the Giant Killer." The Giants needed Matty's best. They had lost a doubleheader to the Cubs the day before and the team was hurting. "How are the cripples?" McGraw asked as he came into the clubhouse. "Any more to add to the list of identified dead today?"

Well, yes, as a matter of fact. Fred Tenney, the yeoman first baseman, had woken up with an attack of lumbago, so McGraw had to put Fred Merkle into the starting lineup for the first time all season. Merkle was a big Wisconsin farm boy who had come up to New York the year before, but he was still only nineteen years old.

But "Big Six," in his greatest season, was up to the challenge, holding the Cubs to just one run. Jack Pfiester had good stuff, too, though, and the wounded Giants themselves had managed only a single run as they came to bat in the home half of the ninth. And here came the most spectacularly controversial inning ever.

With one out, Art Devlin, the third baseman, singled. Moose McCormick — like Mathewson, a Bucknell man — forced him at second, but then young Merkle took Pfiester the other way, lining a single to right, sending McCormick to third. Al Bridwell, the shortstop, then swung at Pfiester's first pitch and laced a clean single dead up the middle. In fact, the field umpire, Bob Emslie, had to fall down to escape being hit by the line drive. He got up and dutifully watched Bridwell run safely to first. The plate umpire, Hank O'Day, saw McCormick touch home for the winning run — 2–1, Giants. New York was back in first place, and the fans poured out of their seats. As one reporter wrote: "The merry villagers flocked onto the field to worship the hollow where the Mathewson feet have pressed."

Matty himself ran out to embrace the happy Merkle and escort the young fellow off the field.

Meanwhile, almost unnoticed, Johnny Evers, the Cubs second baseman, was standing on second, calling for the center fielder, "Circus" Solly Hofman, to chuck him the ball. Evers was a fidgety little guy who stood at no more than five-neet-nine and weighed only 125 pounds. Nobody, including his teammates, much liked him, but he was a heady ballplayer. Also, he had noticed this same situation only weeks before, in Pittsburgh, but had been unsuccessful in prosecuting his charge then. But here it was again: Merkle, the man on first, was required to move up a base once Bridwell hit safely. No matter how quickly McCormick, the runner on third, crossed the plate, if Merkle didn't touch second, then he was forced out, the inning was over, the run didn't count, and it was still a 1–1 tie.

Three different pitchers — McGinnity, Wiltse, and Mathewson — all seemed to have later remembered that they were coaching first. Since it was the first base coach's responsibility to tell the runner to be sure to go down and touch second, it's odd that anyone would claim that dubious honor. Anyway, almost surely it wasn't Mathewson; he was pitching, after all. McGinnity is the likely choice, because only he of all the Giants seems to have caught on to what Evers was up to.

Apparently the Iron Man ran out and wrestled the ball away from little Evers (or from a Chicago pitcher, Rube Kroh — details of the chaos differ in almost every account) and hurled it as far away as he could, into the stands. Maybe there was even a fight. "Fists flew on all sides, eyes swelled up and blood flowed," wrote the *World* reporter. Did a Cub reserve pummel the fan who caught the ball in order to retrieve it? Whatever, undaunted, Evers somehow regained possession of that ball or, more likely, simply produced another, hailed Emslie, stepped on second, and claimed that Merkle was out. Emslie said he couldn't rule; he hadn't been watching Merkle. But prompted by the indomitable

Evers, Emslie asked his colleague, O'Day, if he had seen the play at second. Indeed he had, said O'Day, and, yes, Merkle had turned round on the basepath before reaching the base. Therefore he was now forced out and McCormick's run for the Giants didn't count.

By now the field was overrun with the merry villagers and the early autumn gloaming was coming down. Most everybody left the park believing Matty and the Giants had won. Mathewson remembered that even when the Giants, in their clubhouse, heard about O'Day's call, they at first "laughed, for it didn't seem like a situation to be taken seriously." When they realized that O'Day really had called Merkle out and the game a tie on account of darkness, the mood grew darker. Mathewson was bitter. "If we lose the pennant thereby, I'll never play pro ball again," he declared. Muggsy, of course, was angrier and more profane, snarling: "That dirty son of a bitch. O'Day is trying to rob us."

Poor Merkle was utterly distraught. In the days that followed, Mathewson would write, "He moped. He lost flesh" — twenty pounds — "his eyes were hollow and his cheeks sunken." The kid was lacerated in the press. W. A. Aulick, the *Times* baseball reporter, wrote simply that it was "censurable stupidity on the part of player Merkle." The home fans would hiss upon his appearance on the field. It was, wrote the *Sun*, "a situation that has baseball cranks all over the country by the ears." The "boner," it was called — the Merkle Boner, the dumbest mistake ever made by a player. Never mind that Merkle was only following the fashion of the time. He had done exactly what that Pittsburgh player had weeks earlier, as Evers watched. The Giants' first base coach, whoever he was, must surely have been at least as culpable. The kid was still a teenager, for goodness sakes. Mathewson admitted that, joyously, he had run to him. Mathewson didn't tell him to touch second. McGraw didn't shout it out. In fact, ironically, this was exactly the sort of rule-book intelligence that McGraw was famous for exploiting. And for all the bleatings and threats of the Giants and their fans, even the owner, John Brush, had to admit that "technically" — always *technically,* not "actually" — Evers and O'Day were right.

Harry Pulliam, the "boy president," was once again forced to rule in a Giant maelstrom, and, after a week, he upheld the umpires. Tie game. Terrible hate mail poured into his office. Naturally the Giants appealed to the league's five-man Board of Directors, and they agreed to meet. The Pittsburgh and Chicago owners had to stand down, since their teams would be affected by any decision. The three remaining owners — from Cincinnati, Boston, and Brooklyn — prepared to assemble. Affidavits were called for.

Merkle, meanwhile, was so depressed that rumors of his suicide began to float about. In fact, he did beseech McGraw to farm him out. "Lose me," the kid pleaded. "I'm the jinx."

McGraw was steadfast. "It wasn't your fault, Fred," Muggsy said, consoling him. Indeed, so supportive was McGraw that he gave Merkle a raise for the next season. Of course, it's also true that at some point Merkle either decided that he had indeed touched second or he was prevailed upon to present that testimony. The affidavits from other Giants and from Merkle swore that the kid had regained his senses after he saw Evers calling for the ball and had turned back toward second and touched the base. All the Chicago affidavits, of course, supported O'Day's decision.

On October 5, the three directors — August Herrmann of Cincinnati, Charlie

Ebbets of Brooklyn, and George Dovey of Boston — convened in Cincinnati to review the appeal of Harry Pulliam's ruling. They adjourned at ten-thirty at night, still unable to arrive at a decision.

FIFTEEN

The next morning, October 6, the board met again, and this time they agreed to uphold Pulliam's decision. Since New York and Chicago had finished with identical 98–55 records, the tie game of September 23 must be played off to determine the league champion. (Pittsburgh would finish tied for second at 98–56 with whichever team lost.) Now, however, for one of the rare times in his life, McGraw was infected by a strange indifference. He professed not to care whether or not the Giants played at all. "It's simply a game of squeal," he said bitterly, leaving all decisions up to the team.

The players, too, still claiming they'd been jobbed, were themselves ambivalent about playing, but finally Mathewson led a five-player delegation to see John Brush, who was ill, abed at the Lambs Club. Brush, too, left the decision up to the players, but perhaps when he offered the team a ten-thousand-dollar bonus, principal trumped principle, and the Giants agreed to "imitate Steve Brodie." He was the fellow who is supposed to have jumped off the Brooklyn Bridge on a bet and lived to collect. So: one game, winner-take-all.

Great tales are now told about the Giant-Dodger playoff of 1951, which ended with Bobby Thomson's home run, the fabled "shot heard round the world." In fact, that best-of-three series didn't attract a single sellout. Only 34,320 fans — a mere two-thirds of the Polo Grounds' capacity — showed up for the finale. Famous as it is, that '51 playoff pales before the Giants-Cubs showdown on Thursday, October 8, 1908.

The Taft-Bryan presidential campaign, down to its last month, was completely eclipsed. Wrote the *World*: "In every city and hamlet in the United States that could boast of a telegraph wire, frenzied fandom . . . hung on the ticker yesterday and waited with bated breath."

The *Times* was not to be outdone in hyperbole in explaining the effect of the game on New York. On page 1, it declared: "Perhaps never in the history of a great city, since the days of Rome and its arena contests, has a people been pitched to such a key of excitement as was New York 'fandom' yesterday." Mathewson, who, naturally, was going to start for the Giants, was no less overcome by the impact of this one game. "It stands out from every-day events like the battle of Waterloo and the assassination of President Lincoln," he opined.

Estimates of the crowd that stormed the Polo Grounds ranged as high as a quarter million. Probably it was closer to a hundred thousand, but however many were left outside, at least forty thousand managed to squeeze into the park, filling up the bleachers and grandstand hours before Matty threw the first pitch. Police reinforcements had to be called, and a hundred more "bluecoats" rushed up to Coogan's Bluff. But nothing stopped the crush, not even fire hoses and drawn pistols. Barbed-wire fences were scaled, pushed down. Jane Mathewson, unaccountably carrying their small child into the very heart of this bedlam, was almost trampled, rescued from the mob by a clutch of policemen. Hooks Wiltse needed a mounted police escort to get inside.

Scores of people were injured, and it was probably fortunate that only one man lost his life. That was an off-duty fireman, one Harry T. McBride, who tumbled twenty-five feet from a vantage he had taken at the 155th Street elevated train station. "His vacant place was quickly filled," it was duly reported. Indeed, every telegraph pole that offered any view of the field was climbed by intrepid onlookers. One spectator fell out of the grandstand itself but, luckily, only broke a leg. When attendants rushed to carry him off to an ambulance, he beseeched them not to remove him from the premises until after the game.

The Cubs, of course, needed considerable protection. They were mad enough as it was, as loud and unruly home team fans had encircled their hotel the night before for all hours, seeking to keep up such a racket as to prevent the Chicagos from enjoying any sleep. McGraw then added to their nerves by keeping the Giants on the field beyond their allotted practice time. Frank Chance and Iron Man McGinnity nearly came to fisticuffs as the dispute raged. Later, Chance would be hit in the neck by a soda pop bottle hurled from the stands. Three-Fingered Brown, who was posted to the bull pen, felt that the Polo Grounds on this day was "as close to a lunatic asylum as any place I've ever seen."

Mathewson, meanwhile, tried to keep his composure. After all, he had a secret that he had shared with Jane before he left their apartment. What he told her, simply enough, was: "I'm not fit to pitch today." The long season had worn him down, and when Matty warmed up, it only confirmed his fears. "I never had less on the ball in my life," he would say. He thought the Cubs would clobber him. "I'll go as far as I can," he told McGraw as he took off his linen duster and headed, disconsolately, to the mound.

As it was, Mathewson put down the Cubs in the first inning, and then the Giants lit into Jack Pfiester, the erstwhile Giant killer. When the Giants scored a run, Mathewson sneaked a peek down the bench at Merkle and saw that "for the first time in a month, Fred smiled." Pfiester was clearly on the ropes. He was nervous and bitching at the umpire's calls. But Buck Herzog got caught off first, and Frank Chance didn't even wait for the inning to end. He brought in Three-Finger, and he put out the fire before the Giants could score any more.

And, really, that was it. Mathewson's suspicions were realized in the third inning. Joe Tinker, who earlier in his career had enjoyed no success against Big Six, had then taken to hitting against him with a bigger bat. With that, he had become, as Hooks Wiltse said, "the only hitter I know of had a jinx on Matty." And it was Tinker who made the hit that broke the game open. It was a triple over the center fielder's head. Fans of Matty made excuses that he had told the center fielder, Cy Seymour, to play back, but Mathewson said no, it was just a curve that didn't break. Even then, under normal circumstances, Seymour might have caught up with Tinker's hit, but he lost the ball in the mass of fans who had climbed on up the tower behind home plate. The Cubs scored all four of their runs in that inning. Mathewson was only surprised by "why it took them so long to hit me."

Somehow he held on till the seventh, when McGraw took him out for a pinch hitter after the Giants loaded the bases against Three-Finger. Laughing Larry Doyle, who hit Brown well, was the pinch hitter, but he fouled out to the catcher, Johnny Kling, who cornered the pop-up even as a bottle tossed from the stands whizzed past his head. That was the Giants' last chance.

In the clubhouse, the smile was gone from Merkle's face. "It was my fault, boys," he moaned. He went to McGraw and once again told him to get rid of him.

McGraw was never more stand-up. "Fire you?" Muggsy asked. "Why you're the kind of guy I've been lookin' for for many years. I could use a carload of you. Forget this season and come back next spring. The newspapers will have forgotten it all by then."

And then he slipped away. Matty heard Merkle say: "He's a regular guy."

The Cubs went on to beat the Tigers in the World Series. It would be the last time they were champions, ninety-six years on. And, of course, for Merkle, the newspapers — and everybody else — never did forget his lapse. Yet for all the abuse Merkle suffered for his boner, for all his life, McGraw was right: he was a tough kid. No matter how often he heard someone scream, "Hey, Merkle, touch second base," he never packed it in. Merkle would play another sixteen hundred major league games, making a last at bat in 1926 when he was thirty-seven years old.

On the other hand, no one can be sure how much the ramifications of the end of the 1908 season affected Harry Pulliam. Surely, though, it was a great deal. He was a nervous man, fragile, something of an idealist, and the brutal criticism he endured for sticking up for his umpire obviously told on him. A few months later, in February, at the winter meeting of the National League, there were more disputes where Pulliam found himself in the crossfire. He suffered a breakdown. He returned to the job soon enough, but he seemed more detached and unsettled than ever.

In the middle of that season, on July 28, 1909, Pulliam took a room at the New York Athletic Club. He put on a fancy dressing gown, lay down, and blew his brains out. The "boy president" was thirty-nine years old.

The next year, George Dovey, owner of the Boston Braves and one of the three directors who ruled against the Giants in the Merkle game, spoke with a writer from the *New York Tribune* named W. J. Macbeth. What he told Macbeth was in confidence, but some years later, after Dovey had died, Macbeth published what the owner had told him.

Dovey said that when he and Ebbets and Herrmann were wrestling with their decision, the affidavits were so completely in conflict that the three directors were "up a tree." Then they came to Mathewson's sworn statement. Alone amongst his teammates, Matty told the truth. It cost him another victory and, as it turned out, it cost the Giants the pennant and a chance at the World's Championship. Still, he told the truth.

"Mathewson," Dovey told Macbeth, "swore that Merkle did not touch second base. He said that he . . . embraced Fred when Bridwell's hit was delivered and ran shouting to the clubhouse after the Giant first sacker had run about halfway to the midway."

Dovey then said: "We took all the other affidavits and threw them into the waste basket. Matty's word was good enough for us."

So it was that Big Six didn't get to pitch in a World Series after a season where he had won his most games. Then, that winter of '08–'09, he went back to Factoryville. His kid brother Nicholas, who was nineteen years old, was home from college. The three surviving Mathewson brothers had all become pitchers. McGraw had given Henry, the middle brother, brief, unimpressive tryouts with the Giants, but Nicholas seemed to be closer in form to Matty. Hughie Jennings, McGraw's old Baltimore teammate who was managing Detroit, had even tendered Nicholas a contract offer, but he had decided to enroll at Lafayette College.

Nicholas had gotten homesick and said he had been feeling poorly, and so he had not gone back to school after Christmas. On January 15, he left Matty and his parents and went fishing. On his way back to the house, he gave the two nice pickerel he caught to a family friend. He told the older neighbor that he had always paid him well when he cut their grass, so he wanted him to have the fish as a present.

A bit later, Matty went out to the barn. When he came back into the house, evenly, constraining himself, he told his parents: "I have awful news, but all of us have to remain calm."

Matty had found his kid brother's body in the barn. Nicholas had written a hasty, incoherent note and then shot himself in the brain. That is why he had given the pickerel away.

SIXTEEN

Mathewson's 1908 season of extremes — majesty followed by disappointment, by defeat, by tragedy — faded into, simply, more excellence. He was 25–6 with a 1.14 ERA in 1909, then 27–9 and 1.89 in 1910. He kept winning at least twenty games a season thirteen years in a row, right on through 1914, when he was thirty-three, and then, just like that, his arm seemed to wear out overnight. But for all Matty's personal success, he in particular and McGraw and the Giants continued to be dogged by the most incredible bad luck. Starting with Merkle's lapse, fate seemed almost whimsical for the team.

The Giants, though, in good times and the few bad times, remained the crown jewel of baseball — "the most spectacular team," the *Tribune* rhapsodized, "whose fame has been sung in every household from Father Fan to Jimmy and Johnny and the rest of the male brood, as they lugged to their breasts their first baseball bats." In another vein, Harry Golden, famous for his *Only in America*, would reminisce: "The Giants represented the New York of the brass cuspidor — that old New York which was still a man's world before the advent of the League of Women Voters; the days of swinging doors, of sawdust on the barroom floor and of rushing the growler."

This, of course, was just the start of McGraw's world. He was also everywhere about town, escorting Blanche to the finest restaurants, to Rosie's, to Enrico and Paglieri's, to Mori's; to the theater and vaudeville. Always, he was driven about. Brush gave him a five-thousand-dollar car as a bonus after the 1908 season, and since Muggsy didn't drive, that necessitated hiring a chauffeur. He drank more and grew stouter, to "aldermanic proportions," a friend noted. Muggsy polished his plate. "I always believe in shooting the works," he said. "Can't stop once I start." He was talking about eating on that occasion, but it could have referred to the way he attacked everything in life. Hoping to duplicate his success in Baltimore with the Diamond Café, he invested in two Manhattan pool halls. In one, at Herald Square, his partners were Tod Sloan, the famous jockey, who revolutionized race riding, and a gambler named Jack Doyle. For the other parlor, nearby, his fellow investor was Willie Hoppe, the pool champion, but Arnold Rothstein, the gambler who would fix the 1919 World Series, was a silent partner. Muggsy liked the company of gamblers. Unfortunately, both establishments lost money. Wildcat investments in mining stocks also disappeared. And, of course, regularly he would lose at playing the ponies. At casinos, he loved to gaily dispense twenty-five-dollar chips to all the ladies in his crowd. Florida real estate would be his last, worst gamble.

Moreover, he was the softest touch in town. He'd buy a suit for a down-and-out friend who had a job interview, hire busted old ballplayers for menial jobs around the Polo Grounds — including two sad old future Hall of Famers, Amos Rusie and Dan Brouthers — and always he was a sweetheart target for pals. Eddie Brannick, a Giant employee who was his confidant for many years, explained: "John really had a dual personality. He was a study in human nature. He was tough with tough people and warm with soft ones." Curiously, McGraw always meticulously noted all those loans he handed out into a little account book; but then he would never call in the debts owed him. He gave away tens of thousands of dollars in his lifetime. "I did wonder if the endless loans or gifts would drain his patience," Blanche wrote, "but I'm happy to say they never did."

After all, he was making big money, the highest salary in the game — right up until Babe Ruth and Judge Landis, the commissioner, passed him. In 1909, for example, the Giants paid McGraw $18,000, double what Mathewson played for. By 1916 it was $40,000, then fifty, topping out at seventy. He dressed as befitting a man of means, usually, for some reason, with a fleur-de-lis pin on his tie. He made sure that Blanche was awash in jewelry. When the Federal League came into existence in 1914 as a major league rival to the established two big leagues, McGraw turned down a $100,000 offer without blinking — and that was hard cash in the bank.

Then, too, McGraw's game was prospering, increasing in respectability. By 1910, as cities grew and mass transit improved — especially with electric streetcars — major league attendance had increased to an average of 4,969 per game. It would have been much higher, except that the Giants and several other clubs were still hamstrung by blue laws that prohibited playing games on Sunday, the one full day when the working populace was off. That year the national American sport also gained a further certification, when President William Howard Taft showed up for Opening Day for the Washington Senators.

Apparently it was spur-of-the-moment. The *Washington Post* had noted that morning that "the opening will not be attended by any ceremony." But here to the ballyard came the portly president, with his secretary of state and an army general in tow, and thus, the *Post* declared, did there come about "the auspicious union of official Washington and baseballic Washington." Taft did not disappoint, either. He had been a pitcher in his svelter salad days. Reported the *Post*: "A mighty cheer swept across the crowd as President Taft showed such faultless delivery. . . . He did it with his good, trusty right arm, and the virgin sphere scudded across the diamond, true as a die to the pitcher's box, where Walter Johnson gathered it in."

More important, perhaps, than even this White House seal of approval was a sweeping acknowledgment from the owners that their growing sport now deserved serious, permanent residences. In

1909 the A's moved into Shibe Park, the first baseball stadium to be built of steel and reinforced concrete. In the next six years, ten more such parks would be erected, including Wrigley Field, which stands yet today as a monument to the sustained futility of its inhabitants.

Then on the night after April 13, 1911, Opening Day, a huge fire took down the Polo Grounds. What to do? There was some talk of putting lights in Washington Park, the Dodgers' stadium situated hard by the Gowanus Canal, and playing Giant games there at night after the Dodgers cavorted in daylight. Such a revolutionary idea was abandoned, though, when, of all people, Andrew Freedman came to the aid of his old team. Freedman had become a small, minority part owner of the Highlanders, and he and his partners invited the Giants to share their American League field until a new Polo Grounds could be constructed.

And yes, from the ashes rose a palacial monument to baseball. The new steel-and-concrete Polo Grounds featured Italianate marble boxes around the upper deck, Roman-style pylons, a balustrade with American eagles and coats of arms of the National League teams, all under a cantilevered roof above that was bright blue, while gold banners fluttered in the breeze. Incredibly, this diamond masterwork was ready for the Giants on June 28, barely ten weeks after the conflagration. By the end of the season, when the Giants took on the Athletics in the World Series, the spectacular new Polo Grounds could accommodate thirty-eight thousand spectators, all with seats designated for their fannies. The quaint days of overflow crowds standing on the field of play were all but gone. The new park was actually supposed to be called John Brush Stadium, but it was the same as when New York unsuccessfully tried to turn Sixth Avenue into the Avenue of the Americas. It was the Polo Grounds, and it stayed the Polo Grounds for more than another half century, until after the Giants had fled to San Francisco, until after the Mets had left for the new Shea Stadium, until even then, when they tore the dear old strange place down.

But now, in 1911, John J. McGraw had an edifice to match his own grandeur. "His very walk across the field is a challenge to the multitude," Grantland Rice wrote. And, of course, Muggsy knew it. He could be insufferably domineering. Sammy Strang hit a home run once, but McGraw promptly fined him twenty-five dollars because he was supposed to bunt. "You do what I tell you, and I'll take the responsibility if we lose," he informed his charges. Except perhaps for Mathewson, everybody else operated under his explicit orders. "I think we can win if my brains hold out," Muggsy humbly declared.

Interestingly, Mathewson was coming to the conclusion that there might be more liability in this control than McGraw appreciated. For almost all his career, though, he kept this thought to himself. Maybe it was simply that Matty was otherwise awed by what the Little Napoleon could create just by the force of his personality. "McGraw leaps in the air," Mathewson wrote, "kicks his heels together, claps his mitt, shouts at the umpire, runs in and pats the next batter on the back and says something to the pitcher. . . . The whole atmosphere inside the park is changed in a minute. . . . The little silent actor on the third-base coaching line is the cause of the change." The Polo Grounds was as much his pulpit as his stage, he as much a spiritual force as a theatrical one.

McGraw was fortunate, too, in one major respect. Not unlike the Yankees today, he had the luxury of playing for the moment. With Brush's bankroll, he could buy his way back up to contention whenever the Giants slipped. And although he cried at least once when he traded a favorite player, he never let sentiment get in the way if he thought dispatching one of his pals would help the team. Nevertheless, despite his authoritarian reputation and the additional demands he placed in training his men, most players liked working for McGraw. Casey Stengel, who played three years for McGraw, was an utter disciple. When he was still a bachelor, Stengel would spend many late nights at the McGraws', talking baseball with Muggsy, periodically fixing plates of bacon and eggs while gobbling down raw peas in between. Mathewson said: "On the field, he is the captain-general and everybody knows it. Off the field he is a member of the team and personal friend of every man. Therein lies the difference between other managers and McGraw."

Muggsy took advantage of every weakness, every foible. For some reason, superstitious ballplayers believed that a cart full of empty barrels meant good luck. When his team was in a slump once, McGraw actually hired a carter to drive past the ballpark again and again with a load of empty barrels as his players arrived for the game. From his deaf pitchers, he learned signing and used that for baseball signs. He was a master at knowing how to treat different personalities differently. Wrote Heywood Broun, Matty's bridge partner: "An important part of McGraw's capacity for leadership was that he could take kids out of coal mines and wheat fields and make them walk and talk and chatter and play ball with the look of eagles."

However, Muggsy's supreme confidence betrayed him in one respect. He was convinced that he was so tough and incisive, both, that he could take any scoundrel and control him. Anyway, he liked the test. And he surely saw some of the worst of himself in these difficult types of players. For a prime example, McGraw took a shine to a busher named Art Fletcher because, in an exhibition game in Texas, Fletcher called McGraw, to his face: "The yellow-bellied manager of a yellow-bellied baseball club." Since that was McGraw's kinda guy, he brought Fletcher to the Giants the next year and eventually he became a valued starter in the infield.

Turkey Mike Donlin was, of course, forever a work in digress. Even in the midst of his superb 1905 season, when he hit .356,

Donlin found himself in jail after he pulled a pistol on a train waiter who wouldn't serve him any more liquor and announced: "Mr. Gun talks loud." Muggsy had to bail him out.

Like Donlin, who married a showbiz star and went onstage himself, Rube Marquard, a fine pitcher, was a sometime actor who got romantically involved with his vaudeville costar, the leggy Blossom Seeley. She left her husband for Marquard. It was all very steamy, including a hurried escape out of a hotel room fire escape. McGraw, the Victorian, harrumphed: "Let him get all the free advertising he can, but let him use some sense in choosing his methods." Closer to home, at spring training one year in Marlin Springs, Texas, Marquard got hold of a six-shooter and shot out all the lights on the town theater. Muggsy had to ante up to keep Marquard out of the hoosegow.

McGraw also did his best to lecture Jim Thorpe, the great football player and Olympian, to steer clear of booze and cards, but it was a losing battle. McGraw's greatest nemesis, though, was Bugs Raymond, a pitcher with considerable potential, little of it realized. Even McGraw admitted to defeat here. "I believe that worrying over Bugs Raymond took five years off my life," he said once, and whenever he suffered travails, Muggsy would moan: "Now you know what I went through with Bugs."

Raymond was, essentially, a hopeless alcoholic. Once, when McGraw sent him out to the bull pen to warm up, he took the ball across the street, entered a gin mill, and traded the ball in for drinks. He arrived at the mound, in relief, roaring drunk. Not that McGraw shouldn't have known what to expect. Playing for Shreveport, Bugs made a bet that he could drink two whole bottles of bourbon, eat an entire turkey, and then pitch and win a doubleheader — which he succeeded in doing. Like so many diamond reprobates of the time, he could be quite charming, though. McGraw hired a private detective named Fuller to watch over Bugs, but Raymond soon sweet-talked the dick into his camp. Standing at the bar rail with his "keeper," Raymond would order two shots, announcing: "I'm full, and he's Fuller."

Damon Runyon, who started covering the Giants in 1911, immediately saw a good story. "I can spend a lifetime writing about Matty, and I shall know enough about Bucknell and other aspects of clean living to found a monastery," he wrote. "Or I can breathe freely and hang out with Bugs Raymond and get the money." On one occasion, Runyon asked Bugs what McGraw might have to say to him when he arrived at the park too drunk to pitch. "He'll keep his mouth shut," Bugs snapped.

"The feller won't try to kill you?" Runyon inquired.

"I'll take his head off with one punch," Raymond responded. "And I'll tell you something else. I would've knocked the first Napoleon on his ass, too."

Actually, most of the money that McGraw docked Raymond in fines he would then, surreptitiously, send to Mrs. Raymond. Nothing helped, though. Bugs drank himself to death at the age of thirty, only a year after McGraw finally let him go.

McGraw snooped on his players to try and keep them on the straight and narrow. He had clubhouse spies and bed checks; he would tip the night clerks at the hotel, so that when a player snuck in after hours, the clerk would ask the player to autograph a baseball. McGraw would then have signed proof of the player's guilt. He also would review the hotel meal checks to see what his overweight players were eating. Battling back, one of the chubbier athletes, Shanty Hogan, would have the waiter put down "asparagus" when he ordered pie à la mode. One year at spring training, Hogan arrived in a suit he had bought that was purposely three sizes too big. He hoped thereby to convince McGraw that he was shucking weight. It didn't work. "You still look like the back end of a truck," McGraw told Shanty.

Occasionally, though, it was Muggsy who came a cropper. A catcher named Earl Smith hated McGraw intensely. "That little potbellied son of a bitch," he would mutter. Traded to Pittsburgh, Smith was still camped out there in a hotel when the Giants came to town, registering in that same hotel. McGraw had a black trainer named Smokey, who performed bed checks. Smith trapped Smokey, locked him in a closet, and told all his old Giant friends to go out and raise hell all night.

McGraw had a slow first baseman named Dan McGann, who played several seasons for him in both Baltimore and New York, but after he traded McGann to Boston, there was no love lost. When McGann got caught running out a grounder, McGraw bellowed "Ice wagon!"

at him — ice wagons being famously slow conveyances. Infuriated, McGann came looking for McGraw that evening and found him in the billiards room at the Copley Square Hotel. McGraw knew McGann was a loose cannon — in fact, he would commit suicide a couple of years later — so on this occasion he put down his dukes, hastily retreated up to his room, and locked the door.

And, just for the record, when he was with one of his favorite players, McGraw got off perhaps the best spontaneous inside-baseball one-liner ever. He was walking down the street with Irish Meusel, an outfielder with a weak throwing arm who made up for his fielding deficiencies as a good hitter. As they moseyed along, they were approached by a one-armed panhandler who most politely said: "Pardon me, sir, I had the misfortune to lose my arm."

"Get on your way," McGraw snapped. "Irish ain't got it."

SEVENTEEN

In more than a century of World Series, only two teams have lost three years in a row. That one of them would be the fabled Giants, led by John McGraw with the mighty Christy Mathewson on the mound, seems fantastic, but so it would be in 1911, '12, and '13. Events were not quite so bizarre as those that centered about the unfortunate Merkle, but dramatic they were, and odd, too, the weirder still that Big Six would be somewhat the goat and mostly the fall guy, but always, at the end, the loser.

After chasing the pennant winners of 1909 and '10 as respectable also-rans, McGraw had guided his Giants back on top in '11 with a team that played just to his fancy. These Giants stole 347 bases, a record that still stands to this day. New York ran, literally, ragged, sliding so often that the Giants were constantly having trouble on the road with ripped pants. The team was so worn down near the end of the season that McGraw put in a call to his jolly buddy, Wilbert Robinson in Baltimore, to come join the team as his aide just to lighten the boys up.

Muggsy had also finally found a pitcher who could replace Iron Man McGinnity as the second half of his one-two punch on the mound. This was the unpredictable Marquard, whom McGraw had purchased from the minors two years previous for the unheard of price of $11,000. Since Marquard pitched poorly his first two seasons, he became known as "the $11,000 Lemon," but in '11 he suddenly blossomed, winning twenty-four games to Mathewson's twenty-six and helping Matty lead the Giants to an easy pennant. So then, presto, shades of King Kelly, "the $10,000 Beauty" of 1887, Marquard became "the $11,000 Beauty" of 1911. The sports scribes were running dry.

Connie Mack's Athletics, defending World Champions, batting almost .300 as a team, breezed to an even easier victory in the American League. This not only set up a rematch of the '05 Series, but since Philadelphia and New York were separated by a mere ninety-four-minute train ride, it created an especially intense rivalry, with only New Jersey as an unwilling buffer.

Betting was rife before the opener. McGraw, in fact, was beside himself that his dear buddy, George M. Cohan, dared bet the A's. Action was easy. "Thousands of Philadelphians came to New York with their pockets loaded with money," it was reported. "Every cent they offered was covered at even money." Not only that, but even though both cities had beautiful new steel ballparks with greatly increased seating capacity, there was a mad crush for tickets.

In New York, outside the Giant offices at Twenty-sixth and Broadway, ticket agents employed so-called huskies to stand in the long lines — coffee and sandwiches provided — to buy the pasteboards that could then be scalped. It was a "seething mob" barely held in check by Pinkerton's. Two-dollar tickets were going for at least fifteen bucks. Tickets were also being counterfeited. The night before the opening game, so many fans bivouacked around Coogan's Bluff — resting in makeshift tents and before fires as they waited for fifteen thousand one-dollar bleacher seats to go on sale — that the scene resembled a "regimental encampment." The next day a record announced crowd of 38,281 pressed into the spiffy new Polo Grounds, with thousands more catching glimpses of the game from the Bluff. A hundred scalpers were arrested, including one especially canny fellow who bought a bundle of newspapers and a vendor's cap for two dollars, and then, posing as a newsboy in the grandstand, tried to scalp tickets for future games.

Once again McGraw outfitted his club in spanking-new black uniforms. Naturally, too, he gave Matty the call in the Saturday opener, where he would be opposing his old Chippewa rival, Chief Bender. And indeed it was '05 redux, except that this time the Athletics actually scored a run off Big Six. That came in the second inning, but McGraw attributed that oddity to Philadelphia chicanery. The A's had a little hunchback who served as a mascot and ballboy, and the Giants grew certain that he was pirating their catcher's signals, imputing this nefarious facility to the hunchback's "being near the ground."

Whether this was true or not, to start the third inning, Mathewson prudently changed signals with his catcher, Chief Meyers, and the A's never scored again. The Giants, meanwhile, made two runs and thereby took the Series lead. Mathewson gave all the credit to Muggsy's omniscience. "McGraw's attitude is reflected in the Giants," he declared. "The club is McGraw. Every play made by a Giant has been ordered by McGraw."

It all seemed so the set piece, with Big Six mowing down the A's, that the *Herald* was moved to epic poetry to honor the aging, thirty-one-year-old Matty:

You licked 'em back in 1905;
 you won again today
You had the same old blazing speed,
 the same old fadeaway.
You punched the Mack men full of holes;
 you spiked their biggest gun
You tore the scalplock off the Chief;
 you put 'em on the run.
There's just one thing we'd like to know,
 and so would Mr. Mack.
So tell us, Christy Mathewson,
 are you ever going back?
They tell us pitchers come and go,
 that age will get us all;
They tell us days are near
 when you'll have nothing on the ball.
But the arm that won six years ago
 is just the same to-day,
And the curves that fooled the Elephant
 fool him the same old way.
Here's to you, Christy Mathewson,

and the man behind your back,
And we hope they'll never tell us that
Big Six is going back.

After the Sabbath respite, the Series moved to Philadelphia. Although the smug New Yorkers dismissed Philly as "Smalltown," there was no less home-team fervor there. Not only was Shibe Park sold out, but enterprising neighbors erected actual grandstands on the rooftops that overlooked the diamond. As many as five thousand more fans paid for this vantage. Meanwhile, back in New York, it was estimated that hundreds of thousands congregated in the streets, and at the Polo Grounds and Madison Square Garden, wherever electric scoreboards had been set up to record the action.

Marquard faced off against Eddie Plank in this game. At six-feet-three, Marquard was taller than Matty, but he was skinny and, strangely for a big pitcher, he had the tiniest hands; they were a fascination, even described as "womanlike." Their daintiness did not, however, appear to inhibit Marquard's ability to grip a horsehide; he would win 201 major league games.

The score was tied at one in the sixth inning when Marquard pitched to Frank

Baker, the A's third baseman. Baker was stocky, just short of six feet tall, weighing 170 pounds, a left-handed-hitting farm boy up from the Eastern Shore of Maryland who was what passed for a slugger in these days of the dead ball. Baker had in fact led the American League in home runs, with eleven, but notwithstanding that distinction, he had a career total of but seventeen, hitting what was called a "four-furlong drive" only once every hundred at bats. Nonetheless, attention must be paid. McGraw told Marquard to keep the ball down. Mathewson advised him to use breaking balls, for Baker had singled off Matty's fastball his first time up Saturday.

With a count at one-and-one, though, Marquard got a fastball up — or, as the *Tribune* described it: "The sphere came billing and cooing along about shoulder high." Baker banged it out of the park to give the A's the game, 3–1. Series tied.

If that weren't bad enough, though, John Wheeler, Matty's ghostwriter, lambasted Marquard in a newspaper column signed by Mathewson. Did Matty approve of Wheeler's choice of words? It was never revealed; whatever, Mathewson took the responsibility for writing that "Marquard served Baker with the wrong prescription. . . . That one straight ball . . . right on the heart of the plate, came up the 'groove' . . . [and] was what cost us the game."

Marquard fumed. Connie Mack posted the column in the A's clubhouse the next day at the Polo Grounds. But Matty was back on the mound and held sway. The drizzle that the game started in disappeared and the sun came out, perfect imagery for what was transpiring on the field as the Giants scored a run while, per usual, Big Six blanked the A's. Going into the ninth, he had now pitched forty-four innings against Philadelphia in the two World Series, surrendering but a single run (and that, remember, possibly thanks only to the shifty offices of the wee hunchback). Matty retired the first Athletic in the ninth, too, and then Baker strode to the plate. On a two-and-one count, Mathewson's control deserted him just enough; his curve sailed high and Baker popped it down the Polo Grounds' short right-field line and into the stands — another four-furlong drive.

The stadium fell to shock. The Giants were in disbelief. In the tenth inning, to Matty's dismay, Fred Snodgrass, the speedy center fielder, bent more on revenge than victory, tried to take an extra base and was tagged out by several feet at third. All he was really trying to do was spike Baker. Even more than usual, McGraw growled and cursed at the umpires, meriting an official censure for his profanity.

Worse, in the eleventh inning, Baker got a scratch single, but it was really the Giant fielders who did themselves in with errors; the A's scored twice off Matty and held on for a 3–2 win. Marquard could not help himself from gloating in print in his own ghosted newspaper column: "Will the great Mathewson tell us exactly what he pitched to Baker? . . . Could it be that Matty, too, let go a careless pitch when it meant the ball game?"

But however much the Giants stewed, Frank Baker returned to Philadelphia a new man. Almost at the instant his blast off Mathewson dropped into the grandstand, he was titled "Home Run." By the next game, souvenirs in Philadelphia were on sale: little replicas of "Home Run" Baker's bat, tied with a red ribbon. The reason these lapel insignias could be manufactured so quickly was that a nor'easter had blown in, and a whole week went by before that fourth game could be played.

So long did Jupiter Pluvius rule that the

sister of one of the A's, Rube Oldring, died during this hiatus, but he was able to go home and attend the funeral and return to Philadelphia with time to spare. Mathewson concentrated on checkers to while away the many hours. Even when the rains finally subsided, the diamond at Shibe Park was a quagmire. Whereas modern sportswriters sprinkle their copy with knowing references to celebrities, to movies and television, the common knowledge of the classics held by literate Americans then could be gauged by how often and casually sportswriters referenced ancient allusions. Now, for example, the man from the *Tribune* wrote: "Hercules' task of cleaning out the Augean stables was mere child's play compared to the job confronting Connie Mack's valiant band of hoe and shovel wielders." Sponges, brooms, and sawdust were employed, so that the Series could finally be resumed after a full week.

McGraw figured he had gained the edge, for that meant he could pitch Matty right back again. Not only that, but the Giants staked Big Six to a 2–0 lead in the very first inning. But in the fourth, Home Run Baker doubled to left to start a three-run rally. The A's were jumping on

Mathewson's first pitch, following advice proffered by Connie Mack. Baker drove in a fourth run in the fifth, when he smashed his second double off the fence, one that just missed being a four-furlong drive. Matty gave up ten hits. When he faced Baker again, he walked him intentionally. The fans booed with glee. Then: sacrilege! Matty came out for a pinch hitter. But to no avail. That "celebrated medicine man," Chief Bender, allowed no more New York runs. A's 4, Giants 2. The *Tribune*'s headline actually read: ATHLETICS WIN AGAIN AS MATTY FAILS GIANTS.

Matty *fails! Fails?* Had that awful verb ever been used before to impugn the beloved master? Hughie Jennings, covering the Series for a newspaper, wrote that he had never seen Matty hit so hard. Big Six himself offered no alibi. "I have no excuse to make," he said stoutly.

So tell us, Christy Mathewson, have you gone back?

Well, no, he was far from finished, but it's fair to say that this game in Philadelphia was the first leaf of autumn.

The next day at the Polo Grounds, with Marquard on the mound for the fifth game, the Giants fell behind. Muggsy yanked Marquard, and New York rallied and won it in the tenth when Larry Doyle slid home. It was a most curious ending. Bill Klem was the umpire at the plate. He would go into the Hall of Fame — revered as the "Great Arbitrator" (although players referred to him behind his back as "Catfish"). Klem could also be as imperious as McGraw, if considerably more genteel. "What was that, Bill?" a player asked once when the umpire was slow to make the call. "It ain't nothing till I say," he replied.

McGraw roared once to Klem: "I'll have your job for this!"

Evenly, the Great Arbitrator replied: "If my job depends on that, sir, then you can have it."

In any event, in the fifth game of the Series, when Doyle slid home with the winning run, Klem gave no signal. He had seen Doyle avoid the tag, but he'd also seen that he'd missed touching the plate. Curiously, though, neither the Philadelphia catcher nor Connie Mack protested, and Doyle just walked away. In effect, the Giants won by default.

McGraw, coaching at third, realized what had happened. He asked Klem what he would have called if the A's had chased after Doyle and tagged him. "I would've called him out," he said.

Both of them appreciated that this would have surely precipitated a riot. McGraw thought for a moment. "Well, Bill, I would've protected you," he declared. Too bad it didn't happen; it would have been fascinating to see Muggsy McGraw defending an umpire from a rampaging mob.

The Series returned to Philadelphia the next day. McGraw held Mathewson out, saving him for the rubber game back in the Polo Grounds. It wasn't to be. The A's finished off the Giants, 13–2. When it was still 1–1, in the fourth, Baker started the rally with a single and scored the go-ahead run. His was the best Series any player had ever had — except of course for what Big Six had done back in ought-five.

EIGHTEEN

Jane and Christy's only child, Christopher Jr., was born on October 19, 1906. Under no circumstances were the Mathewsons gadabouts like the McGraws, but thereafter, as parents, they were even more limited socially than the childless McGraws. Nonetheless, in 1911, Muggsy convinced Matty and Jane to come along with Blanche and him to Cuba. McGraw was throwing together a squad to play some exhibitions against the local nines. McGraw's team consisted mostly of Giants — although he couldn't resist bringing Turkey Mike Donlin back for the trip — and while everybody assumed it was going to be mostly a good time, as soon as the Americans lost a game, McGraw acted as if it were the World Series.

When one of his Giants, Josh Devore, who had been out on the town the night before, contributed to a defeat, McGraw fined Devore and raged: "I didn't come down here to let a lot of coffee-colored

Cubans show me up." McGraw and the others cleaned up with bets, though, when Mathewson threw a three-hit shutout to beat a wonderful little pitcher named José Mendez. Matty called Mendez "great," and McGraw said he'd pay fifty thousand dollars to sign him up, but Mendez was black and so ineligible for organized U.S. ball.

Even after two decades, the Cubans still remembered McGraw as *El Mono Amarillo,* and he and Blanche began returning there periodically for the rest of his life. Three winters later the Mathewsons came back with the McGraws, and the four of them had a grand old time, hanging out at Sloppy Joe's and other bars and restaurants, dallying in casinos and at the racetrack. One time, at the Cuban-American Jockey Club, McGraw bet Mathewson head-to-head in a mule match race. It is unclear why mules were racing, but anyway, they were. Mathewson's mule led coming into the stretch, when it suddenly lost interest in the race and started to inspect an open gate while McGraw's mule roared by to the finish line.

"Don't ever bet on mules, Mr. Mathewson," McGraw said, pocketing his bet. "They're not reliable."

McGraw also took his usual delight in watching Mathewson toy with the native checkers champions while Mathewson convinced McGraw to try some golf, out at the country club in Marianao. It didn't take. Muggsy played occasionally, but he always thought golf was an old man's game. It baffled him why healthy young men would fool with such a meager exercise. One time, in Pittsburgh, Mathewson played golf the morning after he had pitched a victory. McGraw surprised Mathewson by calling him in for relief that afternoon. Mathewson was less than stellar, and when McGraw found out that Matty had been on the links that morning, he blew his top and fined him a hundred dollars.

On an earlier occasion, when Mathewson thought a game another Giant was pitching was safely won, he snuck off to the clubhouse and took a shower. When McGraw then called for Matty to come into the game in relief, Mathewson quickly changed back into his uniform but didn't have time to put on his spikes. Hoping McGraw wouldn't notice, he went to the mound in his street shoes, and got a groundout and a strikeout to end the game. McGraw noticed. "Next time, dammit, don't take your shower in the middle of a pennant race," he bellowed.

In fact, though, once Muggsy agreed to let Matty call his own game, there's no evidence that they had any serious manager-player disputes. McGraw distanced himself from his players during the season, but he was Mathewson's bridge partner in spring training and, especially since Jane and Blanche were so close, it was hard for him ever to treat America's idol just like any other minion. Muggsy would never simply remove Mathewson if he were getting hit; it was sort of tacitly understood that Matty would take himself out. Besides, all friendship aside, Mathewson never gave McGraw any trouble, and as much as McGraw prized hardcase scufflers like himself, he had a certain envy for gentle types like Mathewson and Hughie Jennings. But Muggsy admired him even more for his spirit. "Matty has the greatest heart of any ballplayer I ever saw," McGraw said. "I don't think there will ever be another like him for ability, brains and courage." And, at the end of the day, all sentiment aside, Matty was Muggsy's meal ticket. From 1905, when New York first played in a World Series, until 1911, the next time the Giants made it, only three other players stayed on the roster. Matty won for him. "What always amazed me," Blanche said, "was how John could find the answer, the solution, to all his troubles, through victory." Big Six meant victory.

When John Brush finally died after the 1912 season — "he was as tender as a dear girl," McGraw said, using that curious analogy in his touching eulogy — McGraw assumed even more command of the Giants. He was drinking more, though, becoming more irascible, and each spring, in allergy season, his sinusitis — the upper respiratory problems that were aggravated ever after he was hit in the face by the ball that Dummy Taylor threw — grew worse and he more disagreeable. But his reputation only ascended. Not long after Brush was buried, McGraw took to vaudeville, playing fifteen weeks on the Keith Circuit. Mathewson had made a thousand dollars a week two years before. McGraw was paid triple that, making him the highest-paid performer in all of vaudeville. Imagine, if you will, Alex Rodriguez making more for a movie appearance than Tom Cruise.

Bozeman Bulger, the newspaperman who had written Matty's act, did the same for Muggsy. As opening night drew nigh, though, Bulger could not get McGraw to work on his lines. Muggsy finally took the trouble to memorize them just two nights before he opened, showed up at the Colonial Theatre five minutes before he went on, and knocked 'em dead without muffing a word. Dressed impeccably in a morning suit, McGraw told some anecdotes, professed to reveal "guarded secrets of inside baseball as perfected by the Giants," and generally just played himself on a tour that wound all the way out to St. Louis. Sometimes he followed Odiva, the "Goldfish Lady."

The next off-season, McGraw had even grander plans. He would travel around the world, seeing the sights and showing off the grand American game to the heathens. He put a team together, but Mathewson wouldn't go. It was too long a time for Jane and him to be away from Christy Jr. Besides, Mathewson had terrible problems with seasickness, and the idea of crossing the Pacific seemed appalling. So, with a team of players and a battalion of McGraw steamer trunks, Muggsy and Blanche led the expedition across the North American continent and then on to Japan.

"Where Mr. Masson?" the disappointed Japanese inquired.

China was the next stop, then the Philippines and Hong Kong. The tour dipped down to Australia, then back up to India and Ceylon, and on to Egypt, where McGraw conducted a game at the Pyramids. In Rome, the McGraws were granted a private audience with Pope Pius X. Monte Carlo was next, then Paris, where McGraw dined out extensively for being known as the Little Napoleon. Naturally, he visited his namesake's tomb and announced: "I too met the Duke of Wellington, only his name was Connie Mack, instead of Arthur Wellesley."

In London the Americans played a baseball game before thirty-five thousand baffled English spectators, a crowd that included King George. After a side trip to Ireland, the junket returned home on the *Lusitania*. It was estimated that the journey extended over thirty-eight thousand miles. The diamond wayfarers made it back just in time for spring training.

If Mathewson was not quite so intrepid as McGraw, he remained a rock — apparently indestructible even as he moved into his thirties. He peaked with that magnificent season of '08, when he won thirty-seven games, but in season after season that followed he averaged around three hundred innings pitched, twenty-five wins, and under two earned runs a game. Even in his prime his fastball had not been what players call "heavy," and so as speed diminished with age, he did not lose his best stuff. He still officiated quite well enough with the fadeaway and the curve, and, if anything, his control grew even more precise. In 1913 he went sixty-eight consecutive innings without giving up a base on balls.

Mathewson possessed the most supple arm, and early on he had learned how to preserve it. "There was no strain the way he threw," Larry Doyle explained. "He just let loose that easy, country boy pitch of his." All told, Big Six pitched 4,781 innings, and it is almost incidental that he struck out 2,502 hitters, because that was rarely his intent. Rather, his idea was to get by with as few pitches as possible per game.

What Mathewson sought above all was to put the ball precisely where he wanted it, fooling the batters rather than overpowering them. "Anytime you hit a ball hard off him, you never got another pitch in that spot again," said Chief Meyers. It helped, of course, that Matty's supernatural mnemonic skills were such that he would never forget where he'd thrown a pitch that a batter had bested him on.

Mathewson believed control to be the single most important attribute for a pitcher — counting more than speed, variety, or guile (all of which he did possess in spades). Ring Lardner, who in the fashion common to that era liked to write in dialect — his most famous work being *You Know Me, Al* — wrote this about Big Six from an uneducated ballplayer's point of view:

"They's a flock o' pitchers that knows a batter's weakness and works accordin'. But they aint nobody in the world can stick a ball as near as where they want to stick it as he can. . . . I s'pose when he broke in he didn't have no more control than the rest of these here collegers. But the diff'rence between they and him was he seen what a good thing it was to have, and went out and got it."

It was common for the Giants to journey up the Hudson just before their season opened to play an exhibition against the West Point Cadet team. One year up there the subject of control came up, and Matty — always delighted to respond when somebody would put their money where their mouth was — accepted 12–1 odds on $20 that he could not throw twenty pitches to exactly the same spot. Chief Meyers squatted, rested his catcher's mitt on one knee, and simply held it there while Mathewson toed the rubber and, twenty times in a row, hit the target squarely, then unashamedly pocketed $240 of the cadets' money.

As each season passed, though, as Mathewson realized that he must be nearing the end of his career, he was forced to understand that he would be denied what next he most wanted. That was to become the manager of the New York Giants. At least there was no tease; it was perfectly clear that McGraw wasn't going anywhere.

It is a paradox that, whatever the sport, the brightest players — those who would be expected to grow out of a mere game — are often those who never leave. The smart ones begin to see elements that lesser minds fail to perceive, and so they are challenged to move into managerial positions, to plumb new depths of the game. At this time, too, it was more common for the best players to become managers. And, of course, Mathewson had studied at the foot of the master.

Also, his generation had grown up with the game as it had become something more than a game to America. When Mathewson had entered the sport, baseball was, as his father-in-law believed, a disreputable enterprise played by antediluvian ruffians. Stadiums were thrown up like circus tents, and franchises — even whole leagues — moved with the breezes. But now, the whole enterprise was as sturdy as the grand new ballyards, and more and more of the players were couth and educated. Bucknell? Why now, Bugs and Turkey Mike were gone, to be replaced by the baccalaureate likes of Harvard Eddie Grant.

It was a trade-off, though. These better-bred players didn't give Muggsy near as much trouble. Or near as much fun, either. "The men don't get out and fight for the games like they used to," he muttered. "That's what's wrong with baseball." Even presidents lent their prestige to the proceedings now, stadiums were rock-solid, and it had been a decade since a single franchise had been uprooted. The sixteen big league teams seemed to be as immutable as the Ten Commandments, the Seven Wonders of the Ancient World, and the thirteen stripes that flew over America's grand old game. Baseball had become downright hallowed.

There was, however, still one hangover from the old days, an impurity. Fans could get into gambling pools for as little as double nickels a week. You could bet the number of runs, wins, whatever your fancy. A lot of newspapers printed odds. Everybody was betting the national sport, and everybody winked at the fact that maybe some players could be enticed to play a losing game. After all, for all of baseball's success, players weren't making great salaries. Trapped by the reserve clause, they needed off-season jobs just to get by. There was so much temptation. It was instructive that when people realized that Larry Doyle hadn't touched home plate in the fifth game of the '11 Series but no A's protested, the immediate and natural suspicion was that there must be a fix to it.

It was funny. Everybody was always wondering, but nobody wanted to believe what everybody was wondering. It was, in fact, very much indeed the way it would be at the end of the century, when steroids entered what had become known by then as "the national pastime."

In particular, starting not long after he entered the majors in 1905, a brilliant-fielding first baseman named Hal Chase was regularly rumored to be "laying down." But then, Prince Hal was a charming sort. The McGraws lived for a time at the Washington Inn at Amsterdam and 157th Street, and in 1908 Chase, playing for the Yankees then, was a neighbor in the building. McGraw took a real liking to him, and despite the buzz, Chase was made playing manager of the Yankees in 1910. The fox was running the henhouse.

Baseball was simply doing too well for anybody to stop the parade. Why, at some point it even became associated with apple pie.

NINETEEN

The 1912 Series — Giants–Red Sox — came on with such excitement that it eclipsed the hoopla that had made the 1911 Series seem the ultimate. Scalpers were getting $125 for box seats. Three hundred reporters from as far away as San Francisco came to cover the games. The line to obtain cheap seats at the Polo Grounds was longer than ever. Intrepid journalists even uncovered a female encamped midst the male throng. She was dubbed "the mysterious woman in blue" before she was finally revealed just to be one Jennie Smith of Willoughby Avenue, Brooklyn. A large new electric scoreboard was set up in Times Square itself, and it attracted so many fans during the games that traffic had to be diverted. It was the same sort of mess at Herald Square.

Down from Boston for the first game came a band of loyal Beantown fans known as the Royal Rooters. They had been led, dating back to the nineteenth century, even before there was an American League, by a saloon-keeper named Nuf Ced McGreevey — his moniker derived from his habit of certifying a statement with the words "enough said" and then a well-placed spit into the cuspidor. Dressed in red, complete with a large band that played a theme song named "Tessie" and boasting a hundred thousand dollars in betting money, the Royal Rooters descended on Manhattan, where they paraded the enemy turf by torchlight.

The next afternoon before a packed house at the Polo Grounds, the Royal Rooters came on with a snake dance and a cakewalk as the famous Boston mayor John Fitzgerald — "Honey Fitz" — bellowed through a green megaphone. The *Herald* noted, archly, that the mayor "did nothing to attract attention outside of running about the field until they had to hold him in his seat."

Once again McGraw designed new uniforms for the Series, eschewing last year's black and instead dressing his charges in sparkling white outfits with a distinct violet trim. Then, in a decision that displeased Mathewson, McGraw held him (and Marquard) out in order to allow a rookie spitballer, Jeff Tesreau, the chance to start before the home folks. The ploy didn't work; Tesreau couldn't hold a lead and the ecstatic Royal Rooters went home with a 4–3 victory for the Sox ace, "Smokey Joe" Wood.

At Fenway Park the next afternoon, Mathewson was not particularly sharp, and, in concert, the Giants' defense made five errors, costing six unearned runs; after eleven innings, in "the gathering darkness," the game was called, a 6–6 tie. Marquard won the 2–1 makeup game the next afternoon, but when the Series returned to New York, Smoky Joe won 3–1. Back in Boston, Mathewson gave up only five hits and two earned runs, but lost 2–1. He didn't allow a base runner after the third inning, and in the sixth, Chief Meyers told McGraw: "I never saw him have more." But to no avail. Ever since Home Run Baker had hit that four-furlong drive, it was as if Matty was snakebit in the Series.

The Giants were down three games to one now, but Marquard won again, 5–2, at the Polo Grounds, and back at Fenway the Giants routed Wood and tied the Series with an 11–4 win. McGraw snarled: "The Red Sox cracked and broke today." And predictably, the rumors flew that the Sox had given away the last two games so that the Series would go the limit and both franchises would profit with the extra gates.

The game, however, was not nearly so interesting as the events that surrounded it. The Red Sox management, in some fit of idiocy, sold most of the Royal Rooters' regular seats out from under them, catering to rich, new Johnny-come-lately VIP fans. As a consequence the Rooters marched about before the game, stormed the bleachers, and after the game showed their displeasure by rooting for the visitors. "Three cheers for John McGraw and his ball club!" they chanted as the Giant supporters happily waved their blue pennants in joyous surprise.

Not only that, but Boston had won the coin flip, giving the Sox the home field for the deciding game, but the Rooters boycotted the game. Moreover, they were joined in their stayaway strike by many other furious Bostonians, who were sympathetic to how the Royal Rooters had been mistreated. As a consequence, only 17,034 showed up at Fenway, and 1,500 of those had come up on trains from New York. Meanwhile, down in Manhattan, perhaps a hundred thousand or more spilled into the streets to follow the action on the huge scoreboards.

This day, October 16, was a gloomy one, and Mathewson seemed a match for the weather. He was gaunt and withdrawn. One reporter wrote: "As he sat in the corridor of his hotel this morning, it could be seen that he had little left to give. The skin was drawn tightly over the bone on his jaw and chin, and in his hollowed cheeks the furrows of recent years were startling in their depth." The old-timer was all of thirty-two years.

Yet despite Mathewson's dreadful aspect, once the game started, the Sox were "helpless in the face of his speed and elusive fadeaway." The Giants managed a run in the third, and although they squandered several other chances, Big Six took that 1–0 shutout into the seventh. A single and a rare base on balls here gave Boston its first real chance, though, so with two outs, manager Jake Stahl pinch-hit for his starter, Hugh Bedient. The batter he chose was a very ordinary left-handed hitting outfielder named Olaf Henriksen. He had been born in Denmark, but naturally everybody in baseball called him "Swede." Henriksen managed only 487 at bats in seven seasons in the majors, hitting a modest .269. But here, swinging late on a curve, "the confounded son of Thor that he is" (wrote the *World*), slapped the ball down the left-field line. The ball hit the third base sack and bounded far enough away into foul territory to bring home Boston's first run. Fred Snodgrass in center made a nice running catch to end the inning, but now it was 1–1.

Despite the fact that the Giants had routed Smokey Joe Wood the day before, Manager Stahl now called for him in relief. He was a different pitcher this day, however, and New York could not score. For the first time, a deciding game went into extra innings. But then in the New York tenth, the Giants got to Wood. There was poetic justice, too, that none other than Fred Merkle drove in the run that put New York ahead 2–1. Surely this heroic single would erase the memory of his infamous boner. It was only fair.

And so did Mathewson head out boldly for the bottom of the tenth. "Is Mathewson apprehensive as he walks to the box?" asked the *Times*. And it answered: "He is not. And the confidence that was his when the blood of youth ran strong in his supple muscle is his now."

To lead off, as a pinch hitter for Wood, Stahl sent up Clyde Engle, a weak-hitting utilityman. So began the most upside-down inning, where the weak were strong, the strong weak — even if the luck all went to Boston. Down two strikes in the count, Engle lifted an easy high fly to left-center. Snodgrass moved over a couple of steps. "The globe plumped squarely into the Californian's glove," the *Herald* wrote. "It also plumped promptly to the sward." Engle pulled into first. Snodgrass was a fine fielder. No one, least of all Mathewson, could believe it. Uncharacteristically, Matty would "swing his gloved hand in a gesture that is eloquent of his wrath."

In a movie theater in Los Angeles, where the game was being played out by telegraph, Snodgrass's mother fainted dead away with the report of her son's error.

McGraw came out of the dugout. "Stick to 'em, Matty. Stick to 'em," he shouted.

Next up, Harry Hooper. Rattled, Mathewson threw him his pitch and Hooper drove it deep to center. This time, out by the wall, Snodgrass made a terrific catch. Engle went to second. The batter now was Steve Yerkes, a light-hitting second baseman. Unbelievably, Matty, who had walked only three batters in the twenty-eight and a third innings he'd worked in the Series, walked Yerkes on four pitches. This brought Tris Speaker, the "Grey Eagle," to the plate. Speaker hit .383 on the year. He was as considerable a threat as Yerkes had been hardly any. So what happened? Speaker swung at Matty's first pitch and popped a weak little foul fly over toward Merkle, who was playing first.

Accounts differ. Some say Merkle simply froze. Some say he moved to make the catch exactly as he should have. Whichever, and for whatever reason, Mathewson, running toward the play himself, screamed: "Chief! Chief!" That meant that Chief Meyers, the catcher, should catch the ball. Now, for sure, Merkle stopped in his tracks. Meyers lunged but didn't even get his mitt on the ball.

That should have been the third out, the game, and the championship. Two flies to Snodgrass, a pop foul to Merkle. Instead, there was only one down and two men on, and as Mathewson crossed back to the mound, Speaker called out: "Matty, that play'll cost you the Series."

Sure enough, on the very next pitch, Speaker hit Mathewson's curve for a single, bringing in the tying run — Yerkes to third, Speaker to second on the throw in. Mathewson made the percentage move next, walking Duffy Lewis to set up a force play at any base, but it was for naught. Larry Gardner flied out deep enough to right for Yerkes to tag up and score with ease.

In the press box, a tough baseball writer, Steve Mercer of the *New York Globe*, looked down on Matty standing there forlornly, and began to cry unashamedly.

Ring Lardner started to type his lead for the *Chicago Tribune*. It read:

"Boston, Mass., Oct. 16 — Just after Steve Yerkes had crossed the plate with the run that gave Boston's Red Sox the world's championship in the tenth inning of the deciding game of the greatest series ever played for the big title, while the thousands made temporary crazy by a triumph entirely unexpected, yelled, screamed, stamped their feet, smashed hats and hugged one another, there was seen one of the saddest sights in the history of a sport that is a wonderful picture of joy and gloom. It was the spectacle of a man, old as baseball players are reckoned, walking from the middle of the field to the New York players' bench with bowed head and drooping shoulders, with tears streaming from his eyes, a man on whom his team's fortunes had been staked and lost, a man who would have proven his clear title to the test reposed in him if his mates had stood by him in the supreme test. The man was Christy Mathewson.

"Beaten 3 to 2 by a club he would have conquered if he had been given the support deserved by his wonderful pitching, Matty tonight is greater in the eyes of the New York public than ever before. Even the joy-mad population of Boston confesses that his should have been the victory and his the praise."

McGraw, always ready to defend his players, did not blame Snodgrass for the loss. "It could happen to anyone," he said. "If it hadn't been for a lot Snodgrass did, we wouldn't have been playing in that game at all." Just as he had given Merkle a raise after '08, so now would he do the same for Snodgrass. Neither did Mathewson put the onus on his center fielder. He wrote: "I blame Meyers and Merkle for failing to catch Speaker's foul far more than I do Snodgrass for his error." But for most everybody else, almost from the moment Snodgrass let that ball tumble to the sward, he had cost the Giants the championship. Nobody much ever even credited Snodgrass for the terrific catch he made in deep center on Hooper's ball just after he'd dropped Engle's.

After the game, Snodgrass picked up his sweater, avoided speaking to anyone, and, according to Jeff Tesreau, "acted as if he was a criminal." Riding in the taxi going back to the hotel with Tesreau and Josh Devore, he began to cry and then moaned: "Boys, I lost the championship for you." Neither of the other two players protested because, as Tesreau said, without pity, "He really had, and there was no use trying to deny it."

The press was just as hard on him. The *Tribune*'s lead, for example, bordered on the cruel: "The name of Fred Snodgrass is on the lips of the baseball world to-night, for almost alone and unaided he gave the championship of the world to the Boston Red Sox. . . . [The error] will give the New York centre fielder something to think about when the wind is whistling through the eaves and the wood fire is crackling this winter." (Never mind that Snodgrass lived in Southern California.)

Typical headlines the next morning read: SOX CHAMPIONS ON MUFFED FLY OR A $29,495 MUFF BEATS GIANTS IN WORLD'S SERIES.

Over time, the figure was rounded off to thirty thousand dollars — that being the total difference between the winning and losing team shares. The word "muff" became as attached to Snodgrass as "boner" had been to Merkle.

Snodgrass was twenty-four years old in that World Series. He was a better-than-average major leaguer, batting as high as .321 in one season. He was slim and handsome, well liked — his teammates called him "Snow" — and he played four more years in the majors before leaving baseball and going back to California. There, he had a most distinguished career, both as a businessman and a rancher. He was even elected mayor of Oxnard, California. He lived a good long life, sixty-two more years after that World Series. When he died, this was the headline to his obituary in the *NEW YORK TIMES*: FRED SNODGRASS, 86, DEAD; BALLPLAYER MUFFED 1912 FLY.

TWENTY

Some years before, Mathewson had said: "You can learn little from victory. You can learn everything from defeat." Nineteen thirteen only added to his world of knowledge. Once again the Giants won the National League with ease. Once again, they lost in the World Series.

The Philadelphia Athletics were the opposition again, and the excitement in both cities was cresting as high as ever before. The crush for tickets, the scalping; on Wall Street particularly, there seemed to be an increase in the money wagered. The automobile had, by now, assumed control of the streets, and for five dollars (six dollars below Twenty-third Street), a cab would take you up to the Polo Grounds and wait there to bring you back after the game. Along with the customary play-by-play screens around the city, film technology had been advanced to a point where movies of the game could be seen at various Loew's theaters only three hours after the game had ended.

And, here we go again. Home Run Baker hit a two-run homer as Chief Bender beat Marquard in the opener at the Polo Grounds.

Mathewson started the second game, the next day, at Shibe Park. He shut out the A's for nine innings. So too did Eddie Plank shut out the Giants. But for once Big Six caught a break. The Giants were playing terribly shorthanded because of injuries, and late in the game McGraw had to press Hooks Wiltse, a pitcher, into service as a first baseman. It had long been forgotten, but Wiltse's nickname had come, not from anything to do with pitching, but for his fielding prowess when he was a minor leaguer. It "looked like he had hooks for hands." And sure enough, in the ninth inning, when Philadelphia put runners on second and third with no out, Wiltse saved Matty with two spectacular fielding plays.

Then Mathewson himself knocked in the winning run in the tenth inning, and the Giants evened the Series. Searching for new superlatives, the *Tribune* cried out to the heavens that now Mathewson was the "king, emperor and ruler of all baseball pitchers at home and in the dominion of the seas." Shibe Park was in the ocean?

Oh well, by the time Matty took the mound again for the fifth game, Philadelphia had won twice more, and there were even rumors rampant that a depressed McGraw had committed suicide (by cyanide, hara-kiri, or leaping from a window, depending on the version).

The crowd at the Polo Grounds started screaming "Matty! Matty!" as soon as he appeared, but he had something of a shaky start. Baker hit a sacrifice fly, Larry Doyle made an error that let in a second run, and the A's built their lead to 3–0 in the third. After that, Big Six gave up only one more hit. But it didn't matter. "Once more the old master stood out like the Rock of Gibraltar," the *Herald* explained, "but his teammates were like a lot of pebbles on a barren shore." The Giants made only two hits off old Eddie Plank — and one of those was by Matty himself. "Well," Muggsy said, "Matty could hold the A's, but he couldn't hold the Giants."

Mathewson put down Philadelphia in the ninth, striking out the last batter. McGraw was going to pinch-hit for him, so Matty didn't bother going back to the dugout. He just jammed his glove into his back pocket and started trudging out to the clubhouse, beyond center field. It wasn't as tragic as the year before, losing the seventh game in extra innings, but this was the Polo Grounds, this was home, and this would be his Series valedictory. The people stood and applauded and called his name.

The *World* reporter wrote: "They should erect over Matty's grave some hundred years or so from now the epitaph that . . . 'He done his damndest — angels could do no more.'"

As Mathewson reached the outfield, a batboy ran out from the dugout and threw a mackinaw round Matty's shoulders. He walked the rest of the way like that, never looking back, the vanquished warrior, cloaked, leaving the field. As the crowd watched, just before Big Six reached the clubhouse, the mackinaw fell loose from his shoulders and dropped to the ground, but he just kept walking, and then he disappeared from view.

The third straight World Series defeat surely rattled McGraw more than he let on, although it may have taken liquor to reveal the depth of his disappointment. At a good-bye party a few nights after the Series, he suddenly lit into Wilbert Robinson, his dear old pal. Uncle Robbie, coaching at third, had misread a sign from McGraw and sent Snodgrass on a steal. The runner was thrown out. McGraw loudly upbraided Robinson and then summarily fired him. "This is my party!" he screamed. "Get the hell outta here." Robinson responded by tossing a glass of beer at Muggsy as he departed. The two Old Orioles did not speak to each other for another seventeen years.

As McGraw aged, however, it did not always take booze to set him off. In 1915, outside Braves Field in Boston, he not only tripped a loudmouth fan but cursed him, calling him a "yellow cur," and then drew a pocketknife on the downed man before those around him interceded. Never was McGraw more boorish than in 1917 when the Giants lost the World Series for their fourth straight time. The White Sox manager, Pants Rowland, came across the field and most graciously said: "Mr. McGraw, I'm sorry you had to be the one to lose."

"Get away from me, you damned busher," McGraw snapped.

An umpire named Bill "Lord" Byron was a special target for Muggsy. Byron once threw McGraw out of three games in a single series. On another occasion McGraw rushed the umpire on the field, somehow grabbed his pocket watch, and stomped on it. The next day, though, he presented Byron with an even better watch. But Byron stuck in McGraw's craw, and in 1917, in Cincinnati, the day after Byron had thrown him out of yet another game, McGraw confronted the umpire outside the stadium, and after a bitter exchange he clocked Byron. McGraw was very nearly arrested for criminal assault on this occasion, but Mathewson acted as a mediator with the police and McGraw was allowed to leave town, suffering only baseball justice — a sixteen-day suspension and a stiff fine.

Mathewson never seems to have spoken critically on the record about McGraw's rude and even violent behavior. Surely it must have disturbed him, but somehow he accepted that truculence as an excusable outlet of Muggsy's great passion for victory. That wouldn't be unusual; many well-mannered people in sports are often so very generous in forgiving "competitors" the sort of egregiously aggressive behavior that would not otherwise be tolerated. Besides, Mathewson had seen so much of the good McGraw, and it seems that he somehow simply accepted the strange dichotomy in his friend.

Muggsy's generosity was well known, and the fact that he was so intelligent would also serve as a mitigating factor after he blew up. Frankie Frisch, the college man from Fordham, said: "McGraw was night and day off the field." And: "I always thought he was sort of on the genius side." No matter how crude and vicious he could be on the diamond, McGraw could never just be dismissed as a brute. The wise baseball executive Branch Rickey, a sensitive, deeply religious man, even found that away from the ballpark, McGraw was "quiet-spoken, almost disarmingly so."

Demon Rum might have been altering this demeanor, but for most of the many years that Mathewson served with McGraw on the Giants, Muggsy could be attractive company once he changed out of his flannels into mufti. So it was that the one time Matty publicly faulted his manager, it was strictly a professional assessment. Even then it came off in the nature of a backhanded compliment. This occurred late in the 1914 season, when Mathewson wrote an article for *Everybody's* magazine bluntly entitled: "Why We Lost Three World's Championships."

The thesis of the piece was that McGraw was too much in control for the good of the players. "The club is McGraw. His dominant personality is everything," Matty wrote. As a consequence, when the pressure of a World Series came down, "self-consciousness, overanxiety and nervousness weighed on our shoulders like the Old Man of The Sea." In contrast, Mathewson wrote that the A's and Red Sox were loose and able to "stand on their own feet." He even added that the 1905 Giants who did win the championship were a sturdier lot who "had baseball brains" and didn't have to depend on McGraw at that earlier time.

Having made the point, Mathewson quickly backpedaled and put down his teammates. He wrote that the Giants were "not of championship caliber. We have won the last three National League pennants solely because the club is McGraw." He even called his fellows "a team of puppets worked from the bench by a string," which was a pretty damning assessment. Perhaps realizing this, Matty concluded: "I sincerely hope no one will accuse me of poor sportsmanship. I have not squealed; only analyzed the situation from things that I know."

How McGraw reacted, we don't know.

He did not respond on the record — and, of course, however much Matty had taken McGraw to task, he had put down the players even more so. Maybe the two men aired it out on vacation; it was later in that off-season that the McGraws and Mathewsons vacationed in Cuba together.

McGraw probably had more on his mind, anyway. The 1914 Giants had finished second, but lost to the Braves by ten and a half games. Perhaps he realized that his team that had won three straight pennants was unraveling. He himself was growing even more paranoid about the umpires. The Great War had broken out that August in Europe, and at one point the Little Napoleon even announced: "I feel like the Kaiser," set upon by the Great Powers. "It's the league against New York," he wailed. In one game, Bill Klem, exasperated at all the bitching, cleaned out the whole Giant bench. Mathewson, smirking, led a single-file march off the field. Not even bringing back Turkey Mike Donlin — who was broke and mourning the death to cancer of his young wife, Mabel Hite — helped.

Unfortunately, the 1915 season only turned uglier for both McGraw and Mathewson. The Giants plummeted to last place — the only time in Muggsy's career when a team he managed for a full season finished in last place. But even more unexpected was Matty's dismal performance. It was as if a switch had been turned off. In 1914 he had won twenty-four games, with five shutouts. His control was still pinpoint, his durability, at thirty-three, as remarkable as ever; once again he threw for more than three hundred innings. But in 1915 he experienced arm and back problems and won only eight games, losing fourteen. He came back the next year, as McGraw began to rebuild the Giants, but the arm that had pitched forty-seven hundred innings was wasted; Muggsy knew that Big Six was no more.

In July 1916, McGraw called up Garry Herrmann, the Cincinnati owner. It was well known that Herrmann had soured on his playing-manager, the former Giant, Buck Herzog. There were rumors, in fact, that the sinister Hal Chase, the Reds' first baseman, was going to be asked to take over the club. To Herrmann's surprise and delight, McGraw offered up Mathewson as the new manager. It gave Matty the chance to manage that McGraw knew he would never get with the Giants. Matty agreed; even if he had to leave New York, Matty said Muggsy was "doing me a favor." For Herzog, McGraw would give up two other players, as well, Edd Roush and Bill McKechnie. Herrmann jumped at the deal. Everybody was happy except possibly for Hal Chase.

Mathewson cleaned out his locker and bid good-bye to McGraw. They'd been together for sixteen years, almost to the day. Matty started out of the clubhouse. No one said a word. Then he saw that a few of the Giants were dealing cards. So he sat down, played one last hand, and without another word put down his cards, stood up, and left the New York Giants and Muggsy McGraw behind.

On the train to Cincinnati with Roush, Mathewson said: "I'll tell you something, Edd. You and Mac [McKechnie] have only been on the Giants a couple of months. It's just another ball club to you fellows. But I was with that team for sixteen years. That's a mighty long time. To me, the Giants are home. And leaving them like this, I feel the same as when I leave home in the spring."

Ring Lardner wrote:

My eyes are very misty
As I pen these lines to Christy.
Oh my heart is full of heaviness today.
May the flowers ne'er wither, Matty

On your grave at Cincinnati
Which you've chosen
   for your final fadeaway.

In all the years her husband had managed, Blanche McGraw had never made an extended road trip with the team before, but when the Giants next swung west to Cincinnati, she came along so that she and Muggsy might visit with the Mathewsons. As it was, her husband was his usual baseball self — all business — and had no time for her, so Blanche and Jane just up and left the men. They took Christy Jr., who was nine years old, and the three of them headed off for an impromptu vacation in upstate New York.

McGraw was quickly rebuilding the Giants from the last-place disaster of the year before. The team at one point even won twenty-six games in a row, which is still the major league record, but it was a streaky club, and it finished fourth. The players wanted to give McGraw a present in commemoration of the great winning streak and decided to present him with a handsome collection of the works of Shakespeare — surely the most interesting gift ever tendered to an American athletic coach by his players. But the Giants were out of the race by then, so McGraw had taken off to the racetrack at Laurel, near Baltimore. The players mailed him the Shakespeare set.

The joke in Cincinnati was that it had been the first city to have a professional team, in 1869, but unfortunately hadn't had one since. Mathewson wasn't able to change that reputation in 1916, when the Reds tied for the cellar (or tied for seventh place if you saw the glass as half full), but in 1917 he steered them to a fourth-place finish.

However satisfying that must have been to Matty, though, the year was a sad one. His brother Henry had contracted tuberculosis — the white plague. TB is an infectious disease that primarily affects the lungs. It had been the most common serious human infection, and it was often the leading cause of death in America and much of the world. In the nineteenth century, 14 percent of American deaths were attributed to TB. John Bunyan, the seventeenth-century author of *Pilgrim's Progress*, called it: The Captain of All These Men of Death. Before streptomycin and other modern drugs were available in the midtwentieth century, there was nothing to fight TB but rest and fresh air. At best, recovery was only fifty-fifty.

Henry only grew worse, and on July 1 he died in Factoryville. There had been four Mathewson brothers. One had died as an infant, another before he was twenty. Now Henry was dead at thirty. Matty, the oldest, the indestructible, was the only one left.

TWENTY-ONE

America joined the war in 1917, and so baseball's prominent long affiliation with German America had to be modified. Charles Dillon Stengel, for example, had sometimes been known as Dutch; now he forever became strictly Casey, adopting the initials of his more benign birthplace, Kansas City. Players with such names as Hans or Heinie anglicized them. The Giants had an especially large contingent of German-Americans on the team, and since they also enjoyed a reputation for a fighting spirit, they had been nicknamed McGraw's Prussians. Obviously that didn't sit well as American boys were dying fighting the Hun.

Muggsy had accomplished an amazing turnaround, bringing the team up from the cellar to the pennant in only two seasons. So at the Polo Grounds, before the fourth game of the 1917 Series, the Giants marched out carrying the Allied flags, making a great to-do about fighting "the

House of Hohenzollern." For whatever it did for patriotism, though, it did not help against the White Sox, who gave McGraw and the Giants another beating in the World Series.

There was talk during the winter of canceling the 1918 season, but President Wilson wanted baseball to carry on, so eventually a compromise was reached, that the regular season would end at Labor Day. Players, however, were given no exemptions. Many left to work in war industries, in steel mills and shipyards; 255 others would enlist. One of them, Harvard Eddie Grant, would die, cut down in the Argonne Forest.

At thirty-seven years old, Mathewson was well above the draft age, but he did his part, selling war bonds. In April, as the Reds worked their way back from spring training, he stood on a street corner in Tulsa, Oklahoma, and gave this pitch: "Come on up, you folk, and let's start the game. Remember, Old Man Hindenburg's up to bat, and we've got two strikes and one ball against him. Haul out your loose change and help win the pennant in the greatest game ever played, and send that bunch of glass-armed bush leaguers in Berlin back to the bushes."

Matty thought his Reds had a chance to win the National League, and they did finish third, after Chicago and New York, but it was a desultory season, with players being called up, and the stands all but empty. Even the Giants drew only 256,000. Mathewson had another problem, too. Almost from the day he took over the Reds in 1916, he had begun to suspect that his first baseman, Hal Chase, was fixing games.

In retrospect, it is amazing that Chase was still playing baseball. He had been under suspicion as early as 1908, his fourth season in the majors, and along the way he had approached numerous players to help him throw games. He was absolutely brazen. The *Sporting News* itself even wrote that other players would call out to Chase: "Well, Hal, what are the odds today?"

Fred Lieb, the baseball historian, always suspected that because Chase was allowed to continue his blatant behavior, that this encouraged the White Sox to fix the 1919 Series. Chase was basically and obviously amoral. He was also a magnificent fielder — some say, even now, the finest ever to play first base, better even than Keith Hernandez. Indeed, Mathewson's suspicions first grew when he saw Prince Hal botch some easy tosses when the pitcher covered first, ordinary flips that a fielder of his caliber could simply not mess up. Chase was also a pretty fair hitter. At .339, he led the National League in batting average in 1916, Mathewson's first year of managing in Cincinnati.

Personally, Chase was charming, seductive in every sense. It was said he was not above sweet-talking his own teammates' wives to sleep with him. He was handsome, although an illness in 1909 had left his face pockmarked, which apparently made Chase even more disagreeable. He would befriend young players, sizing them up, so that he could then tempt the more impressionable ones with offers to help him throw games. Since he had so much practice at it, Chase was also a master at how he, in the vernacular, "laid down." He would make marvelous plays afield and go for base hits when the game was not on the line, then make almost indistinguishable errors of omission when it counted. It took someone like Mathewson, watching Chase game after game, to see the pattern.

Still, it was late in the 1918 season before Mathewson finally felt confident enough to act. On August 6, at the Polo

Grounds, Mathewson heard that Chase had approached a Giants pitcher named Pol Perritt, trying to convince him to throw the game. Mathewson confronted Chase, and after a terrible argument suspended him for "indifferent playing and insubordination." Despite the fact that Chase was hitting .301, not a single player on the team came to his defense. Garry Herrmann, the Reds owner, supported Mathewson, who then diligently went about the task of obtaining affidavits from Chase's teammates, who testified to his cheating.

Incredibly, it would be John McGraw, Mathewson's friend and the manager of the pitcher whom Chase had tried to corrupt, who would come to Chase's aid and effectively save him from expulsion from the game.

But that betrayal lay ahead. Now, Matty was going to war. After long, searching discussions with Jane, he decided that he could not fail to volunteer for his country. He accepted a commission as captain in the Chemical Warfare Service and stepped down as manager on August 27. Soon he was on a troopship bound for France to join what was called the Gas and Flame Division. Several other baseball players and officials had volunteered for the Chemical Warfare Service, including Ty Cobb, who, at the age of thirty-one, likewise was exempt from the draft.

Matty had always had problems with seasickness. This crossing was difficult, and on top of his *mal de mer,* he fell even more seriously ill, caught in a flu epidemic that ravaged the crowded ship. He landed, weak and still somewhat sick. It did not help, either, that the autumn weather was chilly and damp.

Ironically, too, the Germans were in the midst of failing with their last major offensive of the war. With thousands of American troops pouring into Europe, the hopelessness of the German situation was becoming obvious. Noble as Matty's spirit to volunteer had been, it really served no purpose.

Mathewson was posted first to Blois, then Tours, and then on to Hanlon Field at Chaumont, about 120 miles southeast of Paris. Hardly had he begun classes at Officers Training School, though, when his influenza grew worse and he had to be hospitalized for ten days. Finally released but obviously still somewhat debilitated, he was ready for his training.

The Germans were desperate now and

using poison gas profligately on the battle-field. Mathewson's 28th Division suffered large numbers of gas-related injuries. It was Mathewson's job, after his own training was completed, to instruct troops in how to put on gas masks. The men would be sent into large rooms where gas was released. "We weren't fooling around with simulated death when we entered those gas chambers," Ty Cobb remembered. "The stuff we turned loose was the McCoy." All of the officers must have ingested at least some gas, because it was their duty to be the last to put on their masks.

And then, in one particular drill, there was something of a panic. "Men screamed to be let out when they got a sudden whiff of the sweet death in the air," Cobb recalled. "They went crazy with fear, and in the fight to get out jammed up in a hopeless tangle." Cobb himself had a cough for weeks and lungs full of liquid. He felt that only "Divine Providence" spared him. Mathewson, it seems, missed the hand signal to put on his mask and took in even more of the poison before he could finally snap on his mask and escape. "Ty, when we were in there, I got a good dose of the stuff," he said. "I feel terrible."

In fact, when the armistice was declared on November 11, Mathewson was back in the hospital. Then, before he was shipped back to the States in February, he had the duty to examine ammunition dumps in Flanders, where it is quite possible that residual pockets of gas may still have lingered.

He came home to Jane and Christy Jr. with a wheezing cough. Pasty white and with sweat pouring from his brow, he was diagnosed with chronic bronchitis.

Cobb went back to play for the Tigers. It was as if he'd never been away. He hit .384 to lead the majors in 1919. He could never forget that day of panic at the gas chamber, though. "I saw Christy Mathewson doomed to die," he wrote. "The rider on the pale horse had passed his way."

TWENTY-TWO

Because he had gone off to war, Matty had lost his manager's position at Cincinnati. Given the sudden reversal in the state of his health, he probably wouldn't have been up to the job's demands, anyhow. McGraw took him on as an assistant manager for the Giants, a job Mathewson accepted despite the fact that, of all people, Hal Chase was now a valued member of McGraw's team.

That January, while Matty was still in France, the toothless new president of the National League, an old retainer named John Heydler, who had once been an umpire, McGraw his bête noire, adjudicated Chase's case. The evidence against Chase was overwhelming. McGraw even testified himself that, yes, his pitcher, Pol Perritt, had told him that Chase had tried to get him to throw a game. Perritt's affidavit was introduced. So was Mathewson's. Cincinnati players testified against Chase. But Chase brought along three persuasive lawyers and, without Mathewson there to testify in person, Heydler buckled.

It did not help that, incredibly, McGraw said that he believed Prince Hal's protestations of innocence and wanted him to play first base for the Giants. "Here I am, trying to prove the charges that Mathewson, McGraw's close friend, has made against this man," Heydler whined, "and McGraw is already offering him a job." So Chase was merely found guilty of acting "in a foolish and careless manner," McGraw promptly traded for him, and if Mathewson wanted the job with the Giants, he would have to swallow his pride and accept Chase as a colleague. Matty not only put on a good face, but he lied, telling everyone that he'd certainly never accused Chase of cheating. Those charges, he said, had been leveled only by his teammates.

Poor Matty. He compromised himself this one time, it seems, because McGraw was holding out the promise that he would retire in a few years and Mathewson would succeed him. In fact, McGraw would be almost at death's door before he finally took off his Giants uniform. Besides, like so many others, Muggsy — and Blanche, too — had been enchanted by Prince Hal, going back a decade when they were neighbors in the same apartment building. And, as always, McGraw was convinced that there wasn't a player on God's green earth that he couldn't rehabilitate.

But, of course, Chase was incorrigible. Chase was malevolent. He could not be shamed. Somehow, though, he and Mathewson managed to coexist for the whole year without ever talking to each other. One day at batting practice, Larry Doyle's bat flew out of his hands and hit Mathewson. In fact, he wasn't seriously injured, but the whole team rushed to Big Six's side. Except Chase; he did not move. And, sure enough, soon enough, McGraw began to suspect that Chase was throwing games. Yet even then he could not bring himself to confront him or banish him, and rather even than embarrass him, McGraw simply got rid of him by offering him such a small contract for 1920 that it wasn't worth Chase's while to come back from California. Soon Chase was trying to chat up players in the Pacific Coast League, so that he might resume the fixing business in those precincts.

Even allowing for McGraw's idiosyncratic taste in certain rapscallion players, Chase's ability to bamboozle him is perhaps the most baffling personnel mystery in McGraw's career. Or maybe it is just the ultimate proof of how beguiling Prince Hal really could be — that he could put that much over on that grand old student of men, Muggsy McGraw.

As for Mathewson, after he and Chase parted, forever, at the conclusion of the 1919 season, Mathewson went west to the World Series, where the White Sox were playing his old Cincinnati team. He sat alongside the esteemed Hugh Fullerton, of the *Chicago Herald and Examiner*. Rumors about the fix had already begun to spread. Ring Lardner, emboldened by whiskey, had swayed through the White Sox railroad car, singing (to the tune of "I'm Forever Blowing Bubbles"), "I'm forever blowing ball games." In the press box, Mathewson would take his pen and, on Fullerton's scorecard, circle all the plays he thought were funny. There were a number of them.

Luckily for baseball, the lively ball (and Babe Ruth in particular) came to the fore at this time, diverting attention from the shame of the Black Sox scandal. Meanwhile, McGraw's own presence grew somewhat paradoxical.

On the one hand, never had he been so personally imposing. Gene Fowler, the acerbic columnist, wrote: "There were two 'Misters' on the New York scene in the 1920s, men who were always so addressed, Charles F. Murphy, leader of Tammany Hall, and John J. McGraw of the New York Giants." Somehow he rebuilt the Giants into even more of a juggernaut than his teams of the early 1900s or the 1911–'12–'13 clubs had been. The Giants became the first major league team to win four consecutive pennants, from 1921 through 1924. Finally, too, McGraw broke his string of World Series losses, taking the championships of '21 and '22.

Yet in the face of this success, the Giants were losing the city — and, in a real sense, the sport — to their heretofore poor municipal cousins, the Yankees. Once The Babe showed up in pinstripes in 1920, the whole of baseball was changed. He hit fifty-four home runs that year, more by himself than all but one entire team in the majors. Previously, while most New York newspapers had sent a reporter on the road with the Giants, the Yankees were usually covered by a single traveling pool reporter. Now, the press hopped on the bandwagon. Everyone wanted to read about the home run marvel, the "Sultan of Swat"; everybody wanted to see The

Bambino for themselves. In 1920, as a tenant in the Polo Grounds, the Yankees became the first team in history to draw a million fans. McGraw's team sold 360,000 fewer tickets, and the Little Napoleon seethed.

Even before that, when Sunday baseball was made legal in New York in 1919, the Giants wanted all the best dates for themselves and told the Yankees to find a new residence. McGraw savored the eviction, knowing that there was surely no real estate in Manhattan that could accommodate a new ballyard. When the Yankees announced that they would build their stadium out of Manhattan, in the Bronx hinterlands, Muggsy chortled: "They are going to Goatville, and before long they will be lost sight of."

It didn't happen, of course. Ruth only hit more homers. Much as McGraw might have cringed at this new emphasis in his sport, though, he adjusted to the new strategic realities. The Giants very quickly became one of the top power-hitting teams in the league. Muggsy was no diamond Luddite. But that didn't mean he had to like the new order. A letter Ring Lardner wrote him probably expressed his own feelings as well as the writer's: "Baseball hasn't meant as much to me since the introduction of the TNT ball that robbed the game of the features I used to like best — features that gave you . . . and other really intelligent managers a deserved advantage . . . what I enjoyed in 'the national pastime.' "

Of course, it was not just the new anti-McGraw style of play that upset McGraw. Ruth stole the Giants' thunder. In a very real way, too, Ruth replaced Mathewson as the nation's baseball idol. Once Matty had begun to decline, there really was no single figure to take his place. Cobb in particular was simply too ill tempered to be any sort of a national hero, and no other player had risen to popular heights until Ruth came along. Having himself been so adored, Mathewson probably understood the phenomenon and appreciated why The Babe was so appealing far more than McGraw could comprehend (or admit). "Ruth is what he is," Matty said. "It is his temperament that makes him so valuable to baseball and so worthy of his salary. The mass of people on the bleachers care most for a man whom they can cheer today and jeer tomorrow, and Ruth fits that picture."

It was also the case that Ruth's national popularity developed at a time that came to be called the Golden Age of Sport. The Sultan of Swat was only the brightest sports star in the American heavens. Sportswriters had never been better at yodeling their *chansons de geste,* lifting athletes in several sports to new positions of heroism. Jack Dempsey, the heavyweight champion, and Red Grange, the running back, became celebrated national figures. Big Bill Tilden in tennis and Bobby Jones in golf were the first champions in those two country club sports to become, as the term put it, household names. Even a polo player, Tommy Hitchcock, became reasonably well known. If Muggsy had no place in this pantheon of playing gods, he still remained by far the most famous manager. In his lifetime only Knute Rockne, the football coach at Notre Dame, would begin to approach his celebrity. When the *New Yorker* chose him for its first sports profile, McGraw was lionized as more than just a manager. The magazine wrote: "He is the incarnation of the American national sport. . . . There is no man in baseball more coldly, cruelly commercial than John J. McGraw, manager and magnate, and no man more selflessly engrossed in the game for the game's sake than Muggsy McGraw, baseball artist."

Alas, personally he was deteriorating. His health, especially in the spring when allergies affected his sinusitis, was more dicey all the time. Blanche always felt that he never really recovered from the effects of being hit by Dummy Taylor's throw from the outfield in 1903. He would sit in the dugout in his street clothes, sweating through his Cuban shirt, sneezing and coughing. Sometimes, even blood would flow from his nose. Occasionally he became so sick that he would remove himself from the dugout and manage the team by telephone from the clubhouse. His weight had continued to rise, though, and he had taken on a potbelly, or what was more decorously known then as a "corporation." He weighed as much as two hundred pounds (and remember, he was only five-feet-seven). He also drank more and more to excess. His hair turned white. He didn't reach his fiftieth birthday till 1923, but he looked a decade older.

As the 1920s rolled by, though, if ever he pondered quitting, his health would pick up by the end of the season, and he would be raring to go come spring training. He simply could not bear to tear himself away from the game. *Life without baseball had little meaning for him.* . . . So in 1924 he and Charles Comiskey, the "Old Roman," owner of the White Sox, decided that it was time again to present baseball to the deprived English, show the Crown what it had been missing. As a baseball evangelist, then, Muggsy led another foreign tour. Unfortunately, the British were still no more inclined to cozy up to baseball than Americans were to cricket or soccer. George Bernard Shaw wrote a story about how frightfully boring it was. But Shaw also had a long meeting with Muggsy — oh, to have been a fly on the wall — and was perfectly beguiled by him. Shaw had, he said, "at last discovered the real and authentic Most Remarkable Man in America."

Muggsy and Blanche then went on to Paris, where they set up headquarters at the Grand Hotel, making forays hither and yon, returning to entertain at their grand salon.

Yet as attractive as McGraw could still be with the likes of Shaw, he could, increasingly, also be a mean drunk. He knew that himself. Was he drunk? he was asked after one dreadful dustup. "I must've been, because I never fight unless I'm drunk," he replied. That was not altogether accurate, but it did get to the heart of his problem.

He was becoming the stereotype of what he had always railed against: the red-faced Mick rummy.

Some of the incidents were more than embarrassing. They were brutal. Once in Pittsburgh after a game, already plastered, he arrived back at his hotel suite. He took umbrage at some remark that an invited guest made and, without warning, pummeled him so badly that the man was forced to bed for several days. On another occasion, the Lambs Club suspended his membership for fighting with an actor. Some time later, coming home from the Lambs Club after a night of boozing and another fracas there, McGraw, for some unknown reason, slugged the very friend who was helping him to his door. The man suffered a skull fracture when he fell to the sidewalk. This time McGraw was expelled from the club. There always seemed to be some embarrassing skirmish; Muggsy was probably lucky that he wasn't hauled into court.

Although his last pennant came in 1924, his teams thereafter almost always remained competitive. Most of them finished second or third. Still, the American League had indisputably become more glamorous than the senior circuit. If it wasn't the Yankees on top, it was McGraw's old rival, Connie Mack, who had brought the A's back to preeminence. McGraw was making seventy thousand dollars a year, but he was sicker now and strictly second fiddle to the team in Goatville that had become, proudly, the Bronx Bombers.

McGraw had also morphed into more of a grouch. The modern players were less accepting of his imperial manner, and he in turn had less patience for them. Each year, he decided, they became paler imitations of the noble gods from Olympus who had played the game for the Old Orioles. It is revealing that when his old foe, Ban Johnson, died in 1927, McGraw suddenly had praise for him: "Johnson was a great fighter and organizer." But, of course, his old enemy had been of McGraw's sturdy generation. He made up with Uncle Robbie. The Little Napoleon had even developed the unfortunate habit of often referring to himself, lordly, in the third person. To himself and baseball he seemed nearly eternal. "I'm sort of a permanent fixture," he mused once in 1930, "like home plate and the flag pole."

In retrospect, McGraw probably should have packed it in after the World Series in 1924 — his record fourth in a row. His Giants had whipped the upstart Yankees in '21 and '22, but then in '23, when the Yankees had moved into their new stadium, they turned the tables on the Giants. Ruth hit three home runs. The next year, Washington edged the Yankees in the American League and then beat the Giants in seven games, winning the last in extra innings — just as the Giants had lost the first extra-inning deciding game to the Red Sox with Matty on the mound in 1912.

On the train coming back to New York, McGraw left Blanche and walked back to the car where the team was sitting. There, he put on a brave face, giving a classic chin-up speech. "Hard luck boys," McGraw said. "Don't you care. What's one championship more or less? We've won plenty, and we'll win plenty more. Don't fret about it."

Then he returned to the car ahead, took his seat next to Blanche, laid his head on her shoulder, and began to cry in great gulping sobs.

Life without baseball had little meaning for him. . . .

In 1931 the Giants finished second again, and Muggsy grew sicker. His blood pressure was too high and he was diagnosed with prostatitis. The next year, as always, the spring brought more sinus suffering, and now the prostate troubled him, too. He had to miss a lot of games. Besides, the team was losing; the Giants fell into the cellar. Even Muggsy must have known that nobody was listening to him anymore. After a contract dispute, he hadn't even spoken to his best player, Bill Terry, all season.

On June 2, 1932, in his thirtieth season of managing the New York Giants, on a day when the game was called by rain again, John J. McGraw summoned Terry to his office and asked him if he'd like his job. When he got home, Blanche said: "What are you doing home so early? Was the game called off again?"

Muggsy shook his head. "I quit," he explained to his wife. As with most things, he had not bothered to discuss the most important decision in his life with her. Muggsy was always in charge of Muggsy.

Remarkably, his sinuses cleared up almost right away and he had a wonderful time with Blanche in August, going to the races at Saratoga. That winter they went back to Cuba again.

But the pain was increasing, the malignancy starting to spread. That 1933 season, though, of all things, Bill Terry's Giants won the World Series. It was difficult for McGraw, but he attended all five games, two at the Polo Grounds and three in Washington. The last game of baseball he saw, the New York Giants won the World Championship on a home run in extra innings.

The winter was ever harder for him. On February 16, he went into the hospital, and on the twenty-fourth he fell, mercifully, into a coma. Bess Cregar, Matty's sister, arrived that evening in bitterly cold weather to sit with Blanche and comfort her. Muggsy died the next morning. He seemed so old; it seemed that he had been around forever. But in fact he was still a month shy of his sixty-first birthday.

A huge snowstorm fell over New York so that the streets were hardly cleared for the funeral at St. Patrick's three days later. McGraw rested in a plain casket, holding a crucifix. The cathedral was packed, and despite the freezing cold, the crowd spilled over in large numbers outside. It was reminiscent of the old days at the Polo Grounds, when the overflow stood in the outfield.

TWENTY-THREE

Mathewson was never right again after he was gassed. Shortly after he returned from France, he began catching colds, one after another. They settled into a cough that lingered. "In the summer of 1919 he developed a strange lassitude," Jane said. Maybe that is why he managed to endure Hal Chase as well as he did.

McGraw was one person who, right away, feared the worst. Blanche would hear him get up in the middle of the night, shuffling around, even talking to himself about Matty's cough.

Before the 1920 season began, it was obvious to McGraw that Mathewson was too weakened to be with the team. Big Six appeared to shrink. He coughed more and more and lost his appetite. His weight whittled away to 150. Finally came the truth: he was diagnosed with tuberculosis.

The year before, a hundred thousand Americans had died of it. Before that, the disease had struck a disproportionate number of soldiers on both sides of no-man's-land. The infection is spread either from drinking infected milk or from another person who already has TB. Obviously, Matty had taken it on in France. However, tuberculosis was not necessarily fatal. Branch Rickey, for example, had recovered from it years before. That gave Matty hope, even though it had been only three years since his brother had died from the disease. Practically, though, his system was so weakened by the poison gas he had ingested that he never had a chance to fight the tuberculosis. One way or another, the Great War killed him. He did get ninety-five dollars a month disability while he lived.

The sanitarium at Saranac Lake, near Lake Placid in far upstate New York, was believed to be the most salubrious place for TB treatment. It had brisk, extremely dry air and some of the finest specialists. The Mathewsons went there with hope, but quickly learned that both of Matty's lungs were infected. Essentially, that began the toll of the bells. The doctors collapsed his lung; that brought great pain but no progress. "When a fellow can't read or write or talk and barely move," Ty Cobb said, "it takes a little doing to keep his mind off his troubles."

But, in fact, Matty persevered. "A fellow begins to feel that life is worth fighting for and to realize something of what it means to lose it," he said. "Oddly, a fellow thinks less and less of himself and more and more of others. He has less dread of death. He sees that life is good and that death isn't bad at all — if one is ready for it."

Apparently, the fellow accommodated himself well to that possibility.

McGraw would place long-distance calls regularly, from home and on the road, bringing Matty reports of the team's progress. It was cheering that the '21 team regained the pennant. At the end of the season, on September 30, the Giants held a benefit for Matty, bringing back many of his old teammates to play the current Giants in a fun game before the regularly scheduled match against the Braves. It rained, but fifty-four thousand dollars was raised. The mail was already pouring in to Saranac Lake from all over the United States, often addressed only to "Matty" or "Big Six."

The *Times* was moved to write: "Matty . . . still is the undaunted soul in the life battle he is fighting against the white plague." Big Six had always been portrayed as something of a saint; now began the process of raising the saint to martyrdom.

His condition did improve, too. He played some checkers and began to take a special interest in the physical life of the Adirondacks outside his window. "It is a good old world," he told Jane. He traveled south to New York to launch Christmas Seals and was cheered as the "Saranac miracle."

By 1922 he really was a bit better, and although he remained weak, he began to wander about the area surrounding Saranac Lake. He concentrated on studying flowers, counted sixty-one different varieties, searching especially for his favorite wildflower, the blue gentian. "When I see the gleam of petals in the grass," he rhapsodized, "I bend down eagerly to look and see if this is an old friend." With Jane driving him, he took up quail hunting. He also worked on a board game called Big Six. On one trip to the Polo Grounds, when the crowd spotted him, the fans lost all interest in the great war hero General Pershing, who was there with the baseball commissioner, Judge

Landis, and flocked in Matty's direction.

Mathewson was so encouraged that he thought he might be able to return as a coach for Muggsy. McGraw, though, had another scheme. The woebegone Boston Braves were being sold to a friend of McGraw's, and he arranged for Mathewson to become the president. Jane was opposed to the idea, but Matty went along with McGraw. The Giants were the '23 Opening Day opposition for the Braves, and Manager McGraw and President Mathewson embraced before the game. Jane had a right to be concerned. Matty was really only a figurehead, but he wasn't up to even that minimal task. His condition began to worsen again. Now whenever people would see him, they were shocked by his appearance, gaunt and pale, sure enough another of the white plague's victims.

The Mathewsons moved into an even larger house in Saranac in 1924. It was obviously home for the duration; Christy Jr. graduated from high school there, then went off to Bucknell, to his father's alma mater, class of '27.

Over his doctor's objections, Matty went to the 1924 World Series, as a reporter. It would be, of course, McGraw's last, nineteen years after their first, together. The Giants lost the deciding game to Washington, when Walter Johnson, the Big Train, the man who had replaced Mathewson as the premier pitcher in the majors, came on in relief and shut down the Giants. That was the last game Matty saw, hunched over in the press box, wearing glasses now, a body shriveled, lost under sere and sagging skin.

Still, the next February, Mathewson made it to St. Petersburg to watch the Giants train in the warm sun. Unfortunately, even in Florida he caught cold and returned to Saranac, sicker than ever. Rumors of his death came often now; they were, in truth, only a little early. Matty replied, though: "Just say for me that I'll fan death again. He can't touch me, I'm sure of that."

But as the baseball summer wore on, as he celebrated his forty-fifth birthday, the end drew inexorably closer. Matty dutifully kept a record of his temperature. As late as September 29 it was normal, but then it went back up again. The World Series began on October 7. For the first time in five years, the Giants weren't in it. It was Pittsburgh, at home at Forbes Field, against Washington, Walter Johnson pitching for the Senators. In the fifth inning, word reached the press box that Big Six wouldn't last much longer.

On his deathbed, Matty told Jane: "It's nearly over. I know it, and we must face it. Go out and have a good cry. Don't make it a long one. This is something we can't help."

The fellow, who was ready for death, found it at eleven o'clock that night.

The next afternoon, at the second game of the Series, McGraw sat in a field box with Babe Ruth and Ty Cobb. After all these years of hating one another, Muggsy and the Georgia Peach put their antipathy behind themselves for Matty. McGraw said: "I do not expect to see the likes of Matty again, but I do know that the example he set and the imprint he left on the sport that he loved and honored will remain long after I am gone. Matty was my close friend. His passing is one of the great sorrows of my life. God rest his soul."

Both teams wore black armbands and, before the game, they marched slowly out to stand under the American flag, which was lowered to half-staff. Many in the crowd began to spontaneously sing "Nearer My God to Thee":

E'en though it be a cross that raiseth me;
Still all my song would be,
Nearer my God to thee,
Nearer my God to thee.
Nearer to thee.

Then "The Star-Spangled Banner" was played, but muffled.

Right after the game, McGraw left for New York, where he met up with Blanche. Together they went to Saranac, and then, with Jane, they brought Matty's body back to Lewisburg, the little college town where Matty had gone to Bucknell, where his son was now. Christopher Jr. watched with Muggsy, who was one of the pallbearers, as they lowered his body into the ground.

The simple stone raised there read:

CHRISTOPHER MATHEWSON
1880–1925
CAPT 128 PENN DIV

Nine years later, after McGraw's funeral service at St. Patrick's, his coffin was put on a train to Baltimore, where he would be buried. As Muggsy had for Matty, Christopher Mathewson Jr. accompanied McGraw to his final resting place.

TWENTY-FOUR

The tributes that poured in for Mathewson after his death mostly referred to his character. A classic example was what W. O. McGeehan wrote in his column in the *Tribune*: "Matty was the best loved and most popular of all American athletes. . . . If baseball will hold to the ideals of this gentleman, sportsman and soldier, our national game will keep the younger generation clean and courageous, and the future of the nation secure."

Upon McGraw's death, it would be different. The encomiums then were mostly of a professional nature, rather very much the same as those that had come when he retired two years earlier. "The man whose name is synonymous with games everywhere, even in Japan," the *Times* had said then. Now, at his death, it was Judge Landis commending him for embodying "the virile competitive spirit of baseball." Ty Cobb noted that "he put everything he had into baseball," adding, "the game needs more like him." America needed Matty; baseball needed Muggsy.

It is interesting that when, in 1956, baseball instituted an annual award for pitchers, it was named for Cy Young. Granted, Young won far more games than any other pitcher, 511, but most of those came in the nineteenth century, and he had never been nearly the presence that Mathewson was. Then, Mathewson had been voted into the Hall of Fame on the first ballot, Young in the second election. But by 1956, Mathewson had been dead more than three decades, and the role that Matty had originated and played so well — the all-American hero — had been submerged by sheer numbers. There had been another world war, and even tuberculosis was not nearly the threat it had been. Everything about him seemed so passé. Even the New York Giants were on their last legs; they would disappear from existence in 1957. If only Big Six had possessed the foresight to tell McGraw, when he was dying, to sometime win one for Matty.

McGraw has probably fared better over time. His name is still sometimes invoked as the prototypical tough-guy coach, whatever the sport. Then, too, there have surely been more — and more distinct — McGravian copies around than modern Mathewsons. Earl Weaver, Billy Martin, Red Auerbach, Bear Bryant, Woody Hayes, Bobby Knight, Scotty Bowman, Vince Lombardi, and Bill Parcells are all McGraw's spiritual heirs. Matty, though, was more a creature of his time, a collegian when so few Americans were; a sportsman when that mattered; a muscular Christian rather than a born-again. Of recent vintage, David Robinson, the basketball star who graduated from the Naval Academy, is probably the closest example, but he is a minority, an African-American, who played, even for television, in the obscurity of San Antonio. Then too, maybe the reason Mathewson is so relatively little remembered is that he was one of a kind, for all time, necessarily left back in his time. He was a personal paragon, the absolute best at what was then the nation's indisputably premier sport, playing for the most important team in the biggest city — and not, just incidentally, playing for the manager who was the most controversial sports character in all the land. For all Mathewson was, he was more because of Muggsy. Anyway, never again are those

339

planets going to align themselves.

McGraw is the more difficult to piece together. He possessed so many contradictory elements. As competitive as he was, he must have surely been fighting himself more than anyone else. Muggsy was a self-taught first-generation dropout; a self-made little guy; cocky and mean, but sentimental and generous. Most successful coaches today weren't very good players; McGraw was one of the very best of his time. On top of everything else, when he was young and striving, he had to overcome the most terrible tragedies — just as Mathewson saw a picture-perfect early life shatter into shards as he grew older.

Finally, for all that the two men accomplished together, the harsh truth is that, in the crux, the Little Napoleon and Big Six suffered defeat and anguish more than they enjoyed triumph and joy. Mathewson particularly proves how truly powerless any one great player is in a team sport. We so much expect the great star to carry his team to victory, even though time and again it doesn't work out that way.

And, of course, they both died before they should have, McGraw young, Mathewson far too young. Not much memorializes them, either. A Christy

Mathewson Foundation was created upon his death to raise money for tuberculosis. Ring Lardner reluctantly agreed to be its public relations chairman, even though he hated stuff like that. And then, he died of TB himself eight years later. A splendid, ornate Memorial Gateway to Mathewson was built at Bucknell and dedicated in June 1928. Likewise, a monument to McGraw, a "son of these hills," was dedicated in August 1938 in Truxton when the Giants traveled up there for an exhibition game against a local semipro team. Mathewson went into the Hall of Fame in 1936 with the first class of what are always called "baseball immortals." McGraw went in the next year, immortalized too.

Neither of the widows ever remarried. Jane lived in Saranac, where Matty died, then moved back to Lewisburg, where she met him. She attended the induction ceremonies for Matty at Cooperstown and often went back for those annual occasions. She and Blanche McGraw always stayed in touch and saw one another time and again. Blanche lived out her life in New York. She would go up to Giant games at the Polo Grounds and often even journeyed south to visit the team in spring training. She wrote a loving biography of her husband, making sure to stick to the story that Muggsy was not one bit disloyal to her native Baltimore when he kangarooed out. When Blanche would receive letters asking for McGraw's autograph, she would dutifully clip his signature from old canceled checks.

In 1954, when Baltimore returned to the American League after fifty-two years, she came back to Opening Day for the Orioles. Then, too, three years later, on September 29, 1957, she attended the final New York Giants game played at the Polo Grounds. She was given a dozen long-stemmed roses to mark the sad occasion. Blanche died five years later, at the age of eighty-two, having outlived Muggsy by twenty-eight years.

Jane died in 1967. She outlived Matty by forty-two years. Her son, Christopher Jr., also predeceased her. The same sort of calamities that had beset his father and his uncles fell to him, too. After Bucknell, he became a pilot in the U.S. Army Flying Corps. In 1932, when he was twenty-six years old, he was taking his bride of two weeks on her first airplane ride. The plane rose sixty feet, then crashed. The bride was killed. His left leg was amputated above the knee. Remarried, he was killed in 1950, age forty-three, in a gas explosion at his home in Texas.

Christopher Jr. had no children. So, as with McGraw, there are no Mathewson heirs. All that they both left behind were incredibly vivid numbers and the hazy recollections of the lovely things they accomplished together on the diamond back when the American national sport was just finding itself in New York, and all the innings were in the sunlight.

ACKNOWLEDGMENTS

Of the considerable amount of writings about Mathewson and McGraw, the indispensable biographies are *Matty: An American Hero* by Ray Robinson and *John McGraw* by Charles C. Alexander. *Where They Aint*, the story of the Old Orioles, by Burt Solomon, is just as valuable a history of that whole team and era. Philip Seib's *The Player* is the most recent welcome addition to Mathewsonian literature.

Particularly fun reading are two novels. *The Celebrant*, by Eric Rolfe Greenberg, is the story of a family of Jewish jewelers who become especially involved with the good Mathewson and the evil Hal Chase. *Havana Heat*, by Darryl Brock, tells the imaginative tale of Dummy Taylor, as he joins McGraw and Mathewson on their 1911 exhibition tour of Cuba.

Bob Gaines at Bucknell University and Bill Francis at the Baseball Hall of Fame volunteered help with enthusiasm, and so many librarians at the New-York Historical Society were always quick to lend polite assistance as I tried to pick my way through the dusty old years.

I also must thank Rob Fleder, the editor on my original *Sports Illustrated* piece, and Terry McDonell, the managing editor, whose (wise) idea it was to turn a magazine story into what became this book.

— F. D.

ABOUT THE AUTHOR

Frank Deford's work has appeared in virtually every medium. The author of fifteen books, he is senior contributing writer at *Sports Illustrated*, where his byline first appeared in 1962. A weekly commentator for NPR's *Morning Edition*, he is also a regular correspondent on the HBO show *Real Sports with Bryant Gumbel*. As a journalist, Deford was most recently presented with the National Association of Sportscasters and Sportswriters. Voted by his peers as U.S. Sportswriter of the Year six times, Deford was likewise cited by *The American Journalism Review* as the nation's finest sportswriter.